Switching Sides

An imprint of Gulf Publishing Company
Houston, Texas

Switching Sides

Making the
Transition from
Obedience to
Agility

From One of the Owners and Trainers of the USA's Top-Ranked Obedience Dog, OTCH Sweep

Kay Guetzloff

Switching Sides

Making the Transition from Obedience to Agility

Barker Heeler
An imprint of Gulf Publishing Company
Book Division
P.O. Box 2608 □ Houston, Texas 77252-2608

10 9 8 7 6 5 4 3 2 1

Library of Congress Cataloging-in-Publication Data
Guetzloff, Kay.
    Switching sides : making the transition from obedience to agility / Kay Guetzloff.
        p.   cm.
    ISBN 0-87719-355-X (alk. paper)
    1. Dogs—Training. 2. Dogs—Agility trials. 3. Dogs—Obedience trials. I. Title.
SF431.G865   1999
636.7′0887—dc21   99-37604
                                                 CIP

Printed in the United States of America.
Printed on acid-free paper (∞).

Disclaimer

Dedication

I dedicate this book to our dog of a lifetime, Sweep, a Border Collie. She and my husband, Dick, were partners in the obedience ring for eleven years. As of this writing, Sweep is the most winning obedience dog in the history of AKC obedience. Sadly, while writing the final chapters of this book, Sweep left us to join our other dogs waiting for us at the Rainbow Bridge.

Sweep started her agility career at twelve years of age and finished her AX and AXJ titles before time caught up with her. She spent her last year competing in both the AKC obedience and agility rings. She had almost completed the requirements for her MX when an ear problem forced us to retire her.

Farewell, Sweep. Until we meet again at the Rainbow Bridge, you will run forever in my heart.

U-UD, OTCH Heelalong Chimney Sweep UDX, AX, AXJ
8/24/85 to 6/1/99

Contents

over a Series of Four Jumps, 74. Dealing with Refusals, 76.
Call and Send, 78. To Call Your Dog to You and Then
Send Him on to Some More Obstacles, 78. Change of
Direction, 79. To Teach Your Dog to Turn Right and Left on a
Course, 79. To Call Your Dog out of a Sequence of Jumps, 80.
Call-off, Turn, and Jump, 82. To Run with Your Dog, Call
Him out of a Sequence of Jumps, and Send Him in a New
Direction, 83. Call, Turn, and Send, 85. To Call Your Dog,
Turn Him, and Send Him in a New Direction, 85. The Speed
Circle, 86. Panel Jump, 87. Raising Jump Heights, 87.

Acknowledgments

I would like to thank Billie Rosen and Wendy Hultsman of the Jumping Chollas Agility Club of Phoenix, Arizona, for their help in getting me off to a fresh start in agility. Through their guidance, I successfully made the transition from obedience to agility.

I would like to thank my friends Jann Cooper and Margaret Dunfee for their help in proofreading this manuscript.

I would like to thank Jumping Cholla's member Amber Abbot for taking the pictures for this book.

Finally, my thanks to my husband, Dick, for the many hours he spent helping to make, set up, and move agility equipment and for allowing me to share Sweep's final years in the ring.

Introduction

Before the introduction of agility to North America in the mid-1980s, the only performance event open to owners of dogs of *all* breeds was obedience trials. Many dog owners got their introduction to dog obedience when they took an out-of-control puppy to a local obedience class and turned him from Mob boss into a good canine citizen. If the dog did well in obedience class, and even if he did not, instructors would suggest the owner become involved in obedience competition. For many years about the only game in town was AKC obedience, wherein local kennel or obedience clubs offered obedience trials from coast to coast.

The stated purpose of AKC Obedience Trials "is to demonstrate the usefulness of the purebred dog as a companion to man, not merely the dog's ability to follow specified routines in the obedience ring." (Source: *1997 Obedience Regulations,* American Kennel Club.) Unfortunately, over the years obedience competition has become a highly polished, almost choreographed routine. Only a few breeds really excel—breeds that do not mind doing a million repetitions or that will do anything to please their owners. Freethinking is not an attribute in the sport of obedience.

Even when agility arrived on the shores of North America, it was not available to the majority of dog owners. Competitions were held in different areas of the country, but these were rare and usually took place in large metropolitan areas. Many people did not get a look at the sport until the AKC started offering agility titles in 1995. Before that time, because of the availability of obedience trials, most people did not get involved with agility. It seemed senseless to train a dog only to be able to show once in a while, whereas one could go to an obedience trial on many weekends a year.

When the AKC stepped into the arena, more people were given the opportunity to compete in agility. Kennel and obedience clubs found that by offering an agility trial they could add to the club's treasury. Agility trials were held in places where they had never been seen before and were a huge spectator draw at a dog show. For the owners of the breeds in the also-ran category in obedience and for the owners of breeds seldom seen beyond novice, agility was the answer to their prayers. It soon became apparent that many different breeds of dogs excel in agility. That must be part of the attraction for many dog owners. Finally there is something they can do with their dogs and be successful doing it. It is rare to see an agility dog not enjoying himself, but many dogs in the obedience ring look as if they would rather be someplace else.

The terrier breeds do not see much point in obedience. Disobedience is their forte. However, terriers do extremely well in agility. Agility allows the independent thinker a lot more freedom from the control seen in the obedience ring. Many of the hound breeds also do very well in agility. Like the terriers, the hounds are happiest when they are not under the owner's thumb. "Pillow dogs" also compete with great style in agility, whereas they often have a hard time competing against the larger dogs in obedience competition. Owners of these tiny dogs are becoming increasingly concerned about the safety of their little ones on the group "stay" exercises in obedience. The only types of dogs you do not often see competing in the agility ring are the giant breeds. Agility requires speed and dexterity, for which the giant breeds are not noted. The narrow boards of the dog walk and teeter are not necessarily safe for dogs the size of Newfoundlands. Additionally, agility is one place where owners of mixed-breed dogs can compete successfully against their purebred counterparts.

Is it any wonder then that agility is growing by leaps and bounds, literally as well as figuratively? For the obedience fancier, agility training is just an extension of obedience training. The purpose of this book is to explore the ways you can use your training knowledge to prepare your dog for agility competition. In addition, the information within these pages should guide you along the agility path by giving you some insight into what it takes to become a successful participant in dogdom's fastest growing sport.

Chapter 1

Off to a Fresh Start

Agility competition is a natural progression from obedience. It is much more fun for both dog and handler, but it also has its downside. You can expect to check in for your first run by 7 a.m. at many agility trials, and the trial might not be over until after "last call" at the local pub. Agility makes for a very long day at the dog show. However, at least you do not have to hang around all day only to have your dog lie down on the long sit!

At first glance, agility looks relatively simple. Obedience exhibitors who have never run on an agility course have no idea just how difficult it is to run clean, particularly at the advanced level. In obedience, the same sequences are done repeatedly. No wonder dogs and handlers get bored—not so in agility! The course changes from day to day, and everything happens quickly. In obedience, you have time to regroup between exercises. The only time you can regroup in agility is during the count of five while the dog is on the pause table, if there happens to be one in the class in which you are running. There is usually no pause table in the nonstandard classes. Agility is more than just running around the course with a dog. It is often impossible to keep up with Sport when he is running at top speed. For this reason, directional training becomes very important.

An exhibitor in agility does not have to worry about the judge penalizing him for the dog's slow response to drop or recall. The clock will take care of that. A slow drop on the pause table or a hesitation on the recall can add seconds to a dog's run. Judging in obedience is quite subjective. This is not the case in agility. For this reason it is far easier to earn a perfect score in agility than it is in obedience. Most obedience exhibitors go through their whole obedience careers never attaining that perfect 200. In agility, most dogs get several perfect scores in their lifetime. There is often more than one perfect score in the class, and when this happens the placements are based on the fastest times on the course.

Agility Organizations

Currently five separate organizations offer dog agility competitions in North America. Each has its own set of rules, titles, jump heights, types of obstacles, and point values. Many agility enthusiasts compete in more than one type of event. Because of the different rules for each organization, it is easy to get confused and forget what is or is not a reason for passing or failing with that particular association.

> **You can find greater detail about these various organizations on the World Wide Web, under "dog agility."**

The American Kennel Club (AKC), a household name to most dog owners, started offering agility titles to AKC-registered dogs in February 1995. AKC agility entries doubled yearly for the first few years the AKC offered trials. Because of the availability of its trials, AKC now handles the largest number of participants of any agility organization. The purists look down on AKC agility, believing that the jumps are too low and the courses too slow. However, AKC agility trials are more readily available to the average dog owner unless he happens to live in Canada. The AKC even sponsors two teams—mini and standard—to go to the World Agility Championships each year. Unfortunately, mixed-breeds are not allowed to compete in AKC functions.

Beginning in 1999, AKC started offering the title of MACH (Master Agility Champion). In addition, a veteran's program is to be announced in the future.

The United States Dog Agility Association (USDAA), organized in 1986, is the oldest established agility organization in North America and considered by many to be the premier agility body. USDAA promotes international standards as developed in Great Britain, the basis for the world standard in dog agility. The association offers the fastest and most difficult courses and is innovative when it comes to making up "games" classes. The USDAA offers classes for veteran dogs, allowing older dogs to continue competing in the sport, and allows mixed-breed dogs to compete. In 1999, USDAA lowered its jump heights, but dogs competing at its trials still jump slightly higher than they do with the other organizations.

Other agility enthusiasts formed the North American Dog Agility Council (NADAC) before AKC's involvement in the sport. The focus of NADAC is to promote both the sport of agility and to assist exhibitors who want lower jump heights and safer course designs for their dogs. USDAA courses have often been too difficult for some breeds to compete in safely and successfully. NADAC has an innovative idea for its standard classes. It often reverses the course so dogs can run two standard courses in one day with minimal course changes for the club, which saves a great deal of time. NADAC trials rarely use a pause table in the standard class. NADAC sponsors trials in Canada, as well as in the United States. Mixed-breed dogs are welcome to compete at NADAC's trials, and it offers classes and titles for veteran dogs. Additionally, NADAC and the Australian Shepherd Club of America (ASCA) often co-sponsor agility trials in which qualifying runs in NADAC count toward ASCA titles.

The United Kennel Club (UKC) out of Kalamazoo, Michigan, the nation's second largest purebred dog registry, also offers an agility program. Its jump heights are considerably lower and course times much slower than those of the other agility organizations. It also holds fewer events. The UKC, too, allows mixed-breeds to participate, and it sponsors events in Canada.

The Agility Association of Canada (AAC) hosts trials in Canada.

The Canadian Kennel Club (CKC) has recently added agility to its performance program. However, the Border Collie is not a recognized breed by the CKC and therefore cannot compete in its trials.

In dog agility, there are both standard classes and games classes. The standard classes generally make use of all the agility equipment. These are the A-frame, dog walk, seesaw, weave poles, table, tunnels, and jumps. Depending on the type of games classes, the equipment might only consist of jumps, tunnels, and sometimes weave poles. Some dogs are not able to perform on the contact equipment due to fear or physical problems, so the games classes give the owners of these dogs an opportunity to compete in agility. Each organization has different types of games classes. These courses tend to be faster-paced than standard courses because there are often no contact obstacles, or a pause table, to slow down a dog.

Agility championships are offered by the different organizations. You need to read their rules to see how their championship points are earned.

Physical Fitness

Not so long ago, before my involvement in agility began, I was sitting with an obedience judge watching one of the Dog Agility Regional finals. She asked me if I noticed anything strange about what many of the exhibitors were wearing. Well, I observed, they were very casually dressed compared with what we would expect to see in the obedience ring, but that was understandable considering they were running around often at breakneck speed. Then I realized that many of the exhibitors were wearing knee braces. I have seldom seen that in a regular dog show. Knee problems certainly appear to be a serious problem in this sport. In fact, I know of one obedience exhibitor who went to a Halloween party dressed in shorts and wearing a knee brace. She went dressed as an agility exhibitor!

You might consider agility a contact sport, although it is not supposed to be. You can take the term *contact sport* quite literally. The contact equipment is the make-it-or-break-it part of the sport if your dog leaves the equipment prematurely. Contact with the equipment or your dog can land you on the floor or in the hospital. Even if you are not hurt, making contact with your dog or equipment while in the ring may be cause for elimination.

> **When running with your dog on grass or gravel, wearing shoes with cleats is a sensible safety precaution.**

How Fit Are You?

Agility does require some running and making fast turns. It is possible to have your dog do most of the running, but this requires a very well-trained dog. Handlers with dogs of this caliber are rare. It does look spectacular when you see a dog handled in this manner, but realistically, most handlers do end up running a good part of the course with their dogs.

> **Before you embark on agility competition or training, it may be wise to check with your doctor to make certain you are in good enough physical shape to compete in this sport.**

If you compete in USDAA or NADAC, which offer several games classes in addition to standard titling, you could be running as many as four or five runs with one dog in one day. Not everyone is up to this amount of physical activity. If you are running more than one dog, you need to be in excellent shape.

No Upper Age Limit

Because agility competition is relatively new, many exhibitors who have been involved in obedience for years have just started taking up this sport. The exhibitors now competing are older than one might expect to see in the agility ring. One would anticipate that this sport would be for the young, but this is not the case at all. Many of us prehistoric dog trainers often joke about how we wished agility had been a sport twenty-five years ago when we were younger and fitter.

> **Many people getting into the sport of agility are old enough to have an AARP card.**

How Fit Is Your Dog?

You should also make sure your dog is physically fit to compete. There are many dogs in agility that are overweight and out of shape. This is particularly true with dogs competing in AKC agility trials. Dogs shown in the breed ring tend to carry more weight than those seen in the obedience ring. While it is wonderful to see breed champions performing in agility, it could be dangerous for the dog if it is overweight and out of shape.

> **If you believe your dog is overweight, he needs to be placed on a diet. The following is a trick of the trade. Add one cup of solid-pack pumpkin for each half cup of dog food you withhold.**

If you are truly concerned about your dog's weight, consult your veterinarian about Prescription Diet dog food. It will take the weight off faster than anything that can be purchased at the pet store. If your dog is older and an "easy keeper," you might wish to consider feeding him a reduced-calorie diet for maintenance purposes. In addition, if you are using treats for targeting, then you should cut back on your dog's meal on the days you have been training.

For years obedience instructors have recommended that any dog going into open (CDX) obedience competition be X rayed for hip dysplasia prior to starting to train at the open obedience level. Obedience training is physically far less demanding on a dog than agility competition, so you should follow that same advice.

> **My recommendation would be to make sure your dog has good hips and shoulders before embarking on a career in agility.**

In addition, an eye examination should be mandatory when starting agility training. One misstep on contact equipment could cause your dog to fall several feet. Almost every time I have seen a dog leave the contact equipment prematurely, unless he deliberately jumps off early, it is because the dog looked away from the equipment while he was on it. If your dog does not see well, he has no business being in an agility ring. It is not safe. He could trip over jumps or run into obstacles and get injured. Instead of taking your dog to your regular veterinarian, you should consider visiting a veterinary ophthalmologist, who has had specialized training in diseases of the canine eye.

> **When you start training in agility, remember that physical conditioning is all-important.**

You need to exercise and do stretches. Regular walking with occasional short bursts of running will help you be less winded on a course. In addition, your dog will benefit from more regular activity. It is not fair to him to be a couch potato all week and then expect him to be at peak performance on the weekend. He will certainly be doing more work than you will. Taking your dog out for exercise on a bicycle might be good for both of you.

> **Be sure you keep his toenails short.**

Old Dogs, New Tricks

Older exhibitors are finding it rewarding to compete in agility. We have heard for years that exercise is good for you, that you will live a longer and healthier life if you keep active. The same applies to dogs. Many older dogs get fat and out of shape because all they do is sit on the couch from dawn to dusk with no more exercise than a quick trot around the yard. If you have an older dog that is still active or working in some type of performance event, you may want to consider introducing him to agility. You may find he gets a new lease on life, and you will end up spending more quality time together. It is not unheard of to run a dog in agility whose age is into double digits as long as he is physically healthy and his eyesight is not impaired. Dogs in agility appear to last longer in competition, probably because it is more fun than the boring routine of obedience.

Remember that old age is *not* a disease!

Hard Hat Area

Agility is a labor-intensive sport. In obedience, you never need to move or carry more than three jumps. In the past, people have even grumbled about how much trouble that is. In agility, the jumps are the simplest pieces of equipment to move and use. Very few agility exhibitors own all the equipment needed to run in a trial, and even fewer people have the space. Somewhere between 5,000 and 8,000 square feet of flat surface is needed for a trial. Many enthusiasts belong to a club where much of the equipment is available for use. They just own a few jumps, a tunnel, a table, and weave poles to use for practice between classes. There are many outlets for buying agility equipment, but this can be an expensive proposition.

Agility-related sites on the World Wide Web can steer you to agility equipment manufacturers.

A Note of Caution

Agility equipment is heavy and cumbersome to move. It often takes several bodies to do so. All dogs should be out of the area during all course changes. If someone should trip, or even if a person's hand should accidentally slip, the equipment being moved might fall on a dog. It has happened in the past with lethal results. Do not let this happen to your dog. Never give a dog access to the agility area when equipment is being set up or moved.

You really cannot make an open tunnel. It is almost as cheap to buy the chute of the collapsed tunnel as it is to make it, and you can order the barrel from US Plastics. You can save money by making some jumps out of PVC plastic pipe. They are lightweight and portable. You can do a lot of training with only three or four jumps. If you also include your three obedience jumps, you can set up quite a decent jumper's course for practice.

In addition to single bar jumps, you should consider making a tire jump and a table. All these pieces of equipment can be made using PVC pipe except for the top of the table and the tire itself. (Information about how to make jumps and these pieces of equipment can be found in Appendix B.)

Tunnels are heavy to move around, and some exhibitors have bought children's play tunnels to use at home. Most dogs enjoy running through tunnels and will often choose to take a tunnel over some other obstacle. Therefore, it is a good idea to own one or two tunnels. You will need to be able to call your dog off from a tunnel just as easily as from a jump.

Agility Myths

"Your dog doesn't need obedience training to run in agility."

I was told this repeatedly by agility exhibitors before I got into the sport. This is true. However, to be successful your dog should have some obedience training. The more, the better! Many of the handlers I know who have advanced obedience titles on their dogs qualify more often and get their titles faster than those whose dogs have no obedience titles at all. These exhibitors and their dogs have already become partners and are used to teamwork.

"If you ever correct your dog in agility, he'll never run well again."

Now where have I heard something like that before? At an obedience class, I imagine. Agility is no different from obedience when it comes to having to make a correction on your dog. Any correction should always be appropriate for the dog you are training. No correction should be given if the dog is in the learning phase. If the dog is "flipping you the paw," a correction is acceptable. If the dog has been properly trained and is still making mistakes, a correction may be necessary. My feeling is to use as much force as necessary to get the job done. The only way a dog can understand when he is right is to also understand when he is wrong. Corrections vary! A correction can be the word *wrong,* a gruff voice, a scruff shake, or even an eye-to-eye-and-up-on-the-hind-legs stare-down. Corrections do not necessarily have to be physical, but sometimes a physical correction is appropriate. I once removed my dog from the dog walk when he kept choosing to turn right, when I was going left. My handling was not to blame in that particular instance. My dog had decided where he wanted to go, and he went there three times. I corrected him for failure to come, not for getting on the dog walk. Several people told me at that time that he would never run in agility again, but the correction did not phase him in the least.

"You never work a dog on leash in agility."

Your leash is your steering wheel. Granted you would not train a dog in agility wearing a slip collar. It might hang up on the equipment. However, a leash comes in handy, especially in the beginning. It is a form of control. You can prevent your dog from going in the wrong direction or taking the wrong obstacle. You can easily keep him with you if he is on leash. Many dogs, once they begin to understand the "game," start going through or over the various obstacles even when they are "on break." While it may be pleasing to see your dog beginning to understand what is expected, it is not a good idea to let him start doing his own thing. Remember: This is teamwork, a partnership. He should only take jumps and tunnels when told by you to do so.

"If you do obedience with your dog, he'll never learn to run on your right."

There is no question that an obedience-trained dog is more left-side-oriented. However, he certainly can learn to work on your right. It may take a little more time to teach him to feel comfortable working on both sides, but the benefits of obedience training far outweigh the fact that he wants to keep on your left. I found it took about a year for my dogs to feel comfortable running on either side of me.

Obedience myth: "Agility will ruin your dog for obedience."

I once believed this, but I discovered that agility actually taught my dogs to respond faster to commands. They became more responsive in the obedience ring.

Chapter 2

Learning a Whole New Language

Agility Jargon

If a member of the public was to sit outside the obedience ring for very long, he would think he was listening to a foreign language. The conversation might go like this:

Exhibitor A: "So how was your run today?" (Are they discussing this morning's marathon?)

Exhibitor B: "Well, I had a perfect eight, but he muffed the pickup on the flat and had a no-front on the high, and I ended up with a five."

To the uninitiated, this would be an incomprehensible conversation. After all, people talk about perfect 10s, not 8s. In addition, it would appear that the exhibitors were talking about trucks. Was the pickup wrecked? Then suddenly the conversation seemed to switch to the weather, with talk of fronts and highs.

Actually one exhibitor was asking the other how well his dog had worked! Exhibitor B was telling Exhibitor A that (1) the heel-free figure 8 was perfect, (2) the dog had a bad dumbbell pickup on retrieve on the flat, (3) the dog did not sit in front on the retrieve over the high jump, and (4) he scored 195 out of 200 possible points. Another obedience exhibitor would have no problem understanding that conversation.

> **When you get into agility, you need to learn a whole new language.**

Let's take a look at another conversation.

Exhibitor A: "So how was your run today?" (Ah, this you understand because you have used the term *run* in obedience.)

Exhibitor B: "Well, he bailed the scramble, blew by the chute, and popped a pole. Other than that, he was clean. I'm really pleased with his progress because last weekend he crashed and burned."

How do you translate this?

Was the exhibitor talking about breakfast, with talk of the scramble? Did they get back onto the topic of weather, with talk of blowing? Moreover, what is "popping a pole"? In addition, did the dog get a bath? Finally, it sounded like the dog had a serious accident last weekend. How did he get out of the hospital so quickly?

Actually Exhibitor B was telling her friend that the dog (1) jumped off the A-frame before he reached the contact, (2) got called for a refusal at the collapsed tunnel, and (3) came out of the weave poles. Otherwise, he did not make any mistakes. The previous weekend had been a disaster, so he had shown improvement.

In addition to learning agility slang, there are official terms in agility that you will need to master. These terms describe challenges on the course. When someone in obedience talks about the figure 8, you can immediately visualize two stewards standing eight feet apart, with folded arms, and a dog and handler team heeling around them. The following terms are used to describe challenges on agility courses. You need to recognize them as easily as you do the figure 8. At the novice level, the course will have few challenges, and what few it does have will be minor. At the more advanced level, the challenges increase in proportion to the added skill of the dog and handler.

Call-offs

As you might expect, a call-off occurs when there is an obstacle in the path of the dog that he is not supposed to take. Instead, you have to call him off that obstacle and send him in a different direction. A call-off becomes more difficult when the challenge occurs during a fast-paced sequence of the course. In addition, if the incorrect obstacle is fairly close to the preceding obstacle or if the handler is at a distance from the dog when the change of direction is required, the challenge becomes more complex. You are likely to have a minor call-off on a novice course. This means that an incorrect obstacle is placed a good distance from the previous obstacle. The dog then has adequate time to respond to the handler's call. The incorrect obstacle might also follow one of the contact obstacles, which tend to slow down most dogs, giving the handler plenty of time to call the dog in the new direction.

Options

An option is like a Y in the road. Your dog is at the tail of the Y, and he has a choice of which direction to go. Similar elements to those found on call-offs make an option more, or less, difficult. A high-speed approach will make it more difficult to handle your dog over or through the correct obstacle. An option following a contact obstacle will make the correct execution relatively simple.

Traps

A trap occurs when two obstacles are positioned close together. An example of a typical trap is the placement of the tunnel immediately next to the up/down contact of the dog walk or A-frame. The closer two obstacles are placed to each other, the greater the trap. Traps become even more difficult when there is a high-speed approach to the two obstacles. With minor traps, there are several feet between the obstacles, or there is a slow approach. A minor trap might be having the dog go through the tunnel under the A-frame immediately after the pause table. While the dog is waiting on the table, the handler can move to the correct position to block the dog from going up the A-frame.

Lead Out Advantage

> **The handler of a dog with a solid "stay" is at a great advantage in agility.**

Here is where your obedience training pays off. It is quite remarkable how many handlers cannot get their dogs to stay at the start line or on the table without the handler hovering over them. At the advanced level of agility, it is common to have a major trap, option, or call-off at the beginning of the course and/or after the pause table. A handler who can leave his dog at the start line or on the table and who can lead out ahead several obstacles will be in a better position to handle the control point than the handler who runs with his dog.

Side Switches

A side switch, often referred to as a change of sides, occurs when the course changes direction. The handler may need to move from the dog's right to his left. It is possible to run the entire course with your dog on one side only, but it is tiring for the handler. You would have to run farther than the dog, and that is not an efficient strategy. The chance of "making time" when running a dog on one side only, particularly at the upper level of agility, is unlikely. Therefore, you need to be able to run with your dog on both your right and left sides and to be able to switch sides when necessary during the course.

Side switches can be static, blind, or dynamic, as well as in front of or behind the dog. A static side switch would occur when the dog is on the pause table. An easy course would have the dog running on the handler's left up to the table and on the right after the table. The handler could switch sides when the dog is waiting on the pause table. Most of the time a change of sides on the pause table is done in front of the dog. A blind side switch happens when the dog is in a tunnel. A dynamic side switch occurs when the dog and handler are both in motion and the dog can see the handler changing sides.

Weave-on-Right Advantage

For some reason, many dogs find it difficult to execute the weave poles off the handler's right side. Therefore, many courses are designed to test the dog's ability to do just that. A dog that can execute weave poles on the right is at a distinct advantage on many courses.

Directional Commands

There are several directional commands used in agility. "Go" means to run ahead of the handler. You can use another command to mean the same thing if by using "go" it will be confusing to your dog, because "go" means something different in obedience. "Come" means to return to the handler, or perhaps you might wish to use "here." The command "get out" is used when you wish your dog to move laterally away from you. These three commands are the most commonly used in agility. Some handlers use "right" and "left." The biggest problem with using these commands is that "right" and "left" are only correct if the dog is moving in the same direction as the handler. If he is coming toward you and you need to turn him to your left, you would need to tell him, "Right"! Agility is much faster paced than obedience, so it is often impossible to think that quickly. Many handlers cannot even remember their left from their right in obedience, much less in agility. You are probably better off directing your dog with hand signals and your body language.

Watch Your Language

For years, obedience exhibitors have been careful in the choice of commands they use with their dogs. They know it is important not to confuse their dogs by using similar-sounding words for different things. This same principle holds true in agility. At the beginning of each chapter discussing the various obstacles, the common commands for each obstacle are listed. You would be wise to select a command that comes easily to mind. In obedience, many of the commands you use are words you use daily when communicating with your dog—words like "sit," "down," "wait," and "fetch." Most commands used in agility are not words you use on a daily basis. In obedience, successive commands are issued with seconds between them. This allows the handler to think about what he is about to say. On a fast-paced agility course, commands are uttered one after the other with little time in between them. It is easy to say the wrong word, particularly if the command you have chosen is something you have to think about.

Another consideration is that the name of your dog might be similar to the name of an obstacle or directional command. For example, if your dog's name is Fire, you may not want to use the command "tire." If the tire jump is an off-course jump and you call your dog's name in order to turn him before he reaches the tire jump, he may think you just said, "Tire." This may cause him to go off course. I ran into a similar situation with the directional command "switch." I successfully used this command with my first two agility dogs to indicate I had changed sides on the course. However, when I started running my dog Sweep in agility, I found I could not use the command "switch" with her. It was too similar to her name and caused her to turn in the wrong direction. I had to change the command to "cross," and then I had to remember to use it instead of "switch." This is not easy to do when you have little time to think.

Chapter 3

Food for Thought

There is nothing more exciting than watching a dog flying around an agility course, twisting and turning over and through obstacles. There is nothing more beautiful than watching an animated heeling dog. Dogs like this are the envy of most people. Is it all training, or does temperament enter into it? Do not let anyone fool you by telling you it is all in the training. Some dogs are born heeling fools, and others are born racing through weave poles. A dog that takes five minutes to get up from a nap is not going to be the dog that can run through weave poles in less than three seconds. A lazy dog is unlikely to have the fastest time on the agility course unless all the other contestants incur faults. Some trainers believe in miracles and the dog-training fairy. They believe she will wave her magic wand and change the temperament of the dogs they own. Dogs have different temperaments, and temperament is something you cannot change. Therefore you need to work with what you have.

Similarities Between Agility and Obedience

Agility and obedience require a dog to have a solid "stay" and a quick response to "sit," "down," and "come." In both sports, teamwork makes the difference between an outstanding run and a bust.

In both agility and obedience, you may not carry food or toys in the ring. This becomes an issue for those trainers who never wean their dogs off the lure they used initially to shape their dogs' performance.

Differences Between Obedience and Agility

Once you walk in the obedience ring, you probably become a very different person from the one with whom the dog is used to living. In obedience trials, you must use one command only during each exercise. You may give no encouragement if your dog starts falling apart. You may not communicate with him verbally if you want to let him know he is working well, except between exercises. In agility you may use as many commands as you wish and as much encouragement as your dog needs. No wonder dogs enjoy agility so much more than obedience. Many dogs are used to their owners communicating with them all day long. When they walk into an obedience ring and their leaders suddenly become mute, what are the dogs supposed to think? Probably that they have done something wrong. Then they get upset and fall apart. In agility, you show as you train.

In obedience, your dog works on your left side. In agility, your dog works equally on your right and your left.

> **When you take your dog out with you, on leash, start getting him used to walking on your right.**

In obedience, it is customary to use your dog's name before a command. In agility you will rarely have time to say "Sport, jump." You will find it necessary to use the shortest command possible.

In obedience, the only time you may touch your dog is to praise him between exercises. In agility, you may physically "sit" or "down" your dog at the start line, but then if you touch him once he is on the course and before you cross the finish line, you will face elimination.

In obedience, you may not wear any form of identification in the ring. In agility, you may wear a shirt showing club affiliation and displaying your dog's name.

The greatest difference between agility and obedience trials is that in agility you may walk off the course at any time during your run. In obedience, you are required by the Obedience Regulations to stay in the ring until the bitter end. Obedience exhibitors would welcome having the choice of staying or leaving if their dogs are having a particularly bad performance. The reason for this is that the worst thing you can do as a trainer is to allow your dog to continue making mistakes. In agility, if your dog is having a problem, all you have to do is turn to the judge, say, "Thank you" with a smile, and leave the course.

Understanding Lures and Rewards

Today's enlightened trainers use lures and rewards when training their dogs. However, some trainers never get past the lure stage of training. When you introduce a dog to a new command, you lure him into doing what you want. You could prod and pull him, the way training was done in the past. You would eventually teach him the exercise, but at what cost? Dogs learn faster, and enjoy their training more, if you use positive reinforcement. The use of a lure is positive reinforcement.

A lure usually consists of food or a toy—a motivator, if you will. A simplified explanation follows. You hold the motivator in front of your dog and move it in the direction you want the dog to go. For example, in obedience when you want to teach the dog to come to you, you hold the motivator out in front of your body. You draw your hands toward your body to lure the dog toward you. When he reaches you, he gets to eat the treat or play with the toy for making the correct response. If you want the dog to lie down, you hold the lure in front of the dog's nose and move it toward the ground between his front legs. With luck, the dog will lie down. He then gets to play with the toy or eat the treat. In agility, if you want the dog to pause on the contact, you might place food on the ramp. If you want the dog to run through the tunnel, you might place his motivator at the exit. Eventually you expect your dog to respond to the command "tunnel" without the use of a lure.

A lure is used only in the teaching phase. After a number of repetitions of the command, the lure is removed. When the dog responds correctly to the command, he is then rewarded for correct performance. The point at which you move from the lure to the reward is where some trainers go wrong. They never move beyond the lure part of training. Take a look at how you might teach the "down" command. Let's say the dog responds correctly to the command "down" when you hold the motivator in front of his nose and move it toward the ground between his front legs. When you think he understands that he should lie down on command, remove the lure. If you are using food, put the food in your mouth. If you are using a toy, put it in your pocket. However, have the motivator readily available to use as a reward. If your dog responds to the "down" command, immediately reward him. Get the toy out and play with him, or take the food from your mouth and give it to him. Do not pretend you have food or a toy in your hand and use your hand as a lure instead. This teaches your dog nothing. If your dog sits there like a dummy once you remove the lure, you can physically help him into the "down" position. Once he is down, reward him. Go back to using the lure because you may not have done enough repetitions for him to understand what you want. Try the command later without using a lure. When your dog responds correctly to the command, he gets his reward. Eventually put your dog on a random schedule of reinforcement. This means that you do not reward him every time he responds to a command. You might only reward his best performances.

With the use of a reward, you will be able to let your dog know when he has performed correctly. You also need to be able to let your dog know when he is wrong. This is where a correction comes into play. Oh, yes, it's an ugly word—but one that needs to be addressed. Unfortunately, some trainers consider *any* form of correction wrong. This probably dates back to a time when dogs were corrected before they thoroughly understood what was expected of them. Back in those days, corrections were often harsh and unfair. Some trainers still believe that if you make a correction, it has to be something physical. In fact, a correction can be as mild as saying a word like "boo-boo." Sometimes a correction might need to be physical. A lot depends on the personality of the dog you are training. I hope that by the time you get into agility you know with which type of dog you are dealing. Many dogs have a better attitude about training in agility than they do in obedience, so you may need to use a different form of correction to get your point across to your dog.

If you believe your dog knows a command and he does not respond, then you may need to correct him. You must be the judge of what you need to do. Typically, if a dog leaves the contact prematurely, you will replace him on the contact. Although you can hardly call that a correction, by your action you have shown your dog he was wrong. If your dog lies down on the "sit stay" and you return and pull him to his feet, that is a mild correction. If you simply return and tell him, "Sit!" then he will never understand he made a mistake.

Dogs Are Context-oriented

When you trained your dog in utility, you probably discovered that a dog that can do go-outs to baby gates might not be able to do them to solid walls or poles without additional training. Agility is similar in this regard. Dogs may refuse to jump through a different tire than the one to which they have become accustomed. They may not enter the weave poles if they are striped differently or have a wider base. I call this being "context-oriented." The more exposure your dog gets to different agility equipment, the more likely he is to get a clean run.

How Well Does Your Dog Listen at Home?

> One of the reasons I believe many dogs fail in the obedience ring is because they are only "ring-trained."

Does your dog's behavior at home have any relationship on his ring performances? Absolutely! Stop and think for a minute. Does your dog come the instant you call him when you are not actively training him? If you are lying on the bed and you tell him, "Down," does he respond immediately, or will he jump up on the bed before he lies down? If someone comes to your door and you tell your dog, "Stay!" while you go to answer it, does he remain where you left him, or does he stay momentarily and then go to greet the visitor?

Many trainers only expect obedience inside the ring, but a properly trained dog should respond to any command 24 hours a day. Dog training is black and white; there is no gray area. Instant response to a command is imperative in agility. A dog that takes just one extra stride before responding to the command "come" may easily go off course or incur a refusal. This would not have happened had he responded just one step sooner.

As a test of your dog's response to "come," "down," "sit," and "stay," spend several days doing the following. It may take some conscious thought on your part at first, but it might enable you to see that your dog is not as responsive as you thought he was.

Take your dog for a walk off leash, or if that is out of the question, go out in the backyard with him and let him run around. Tell him only once to "come," and that is all. Does he respond? Does he respond quickly? Do not lure him with a motivator, but reward him if he responds correctly. Do this a number of times over several days. Is his response 100 percent, 80 percent, 50 percent? If it is not 100 percent, then you have some work to do on the recall.

Up your demands. Take a favorite toy out with you and throw it for him a couple of times. Then throw it once more, but as he starts out after the toy, call him back. Does he respond, or does he keep going? Remember, once you get into agility you will eventually need to call him off an obstacle in his path.

You have probably worked on random "downs" when training for open obedience. This most likely took place in a formal atmosphere. Did you also practice when you were sitting in a chair, lying on the bed, or getting in the car? Think of ways to surprise your dog by giving him the "down" command when he is least expecting it, but be in a position to follow through and enforce the command to "down" if he ignores you.

I am sure your dog sits for his supper, but does he sit when you let him out of the car, or does he run off to anoint the nearest tree? Dogs are creatures of habit. When you open the car door and your dog jumps out, try telling him to sit just as he takes off for the house or the lake. A "sit" taken out of context may not be something he understands. You probably stopped telling him to sit during heeling a long time ago.

The final test is on "stay." Does he really know what it means? Do not make this a *formal* "stay." When you see him sitting or lying down somewhere in the house, say, "Stay." Then go and do something you know the dog will want to join in. Does he stay put? One test I do is to leave my dog in a casual "stay" in the house, go out the back door, and walk to the front door. Then I ring the doorbell. Not many dogs can resist that. If your dog has been told to stay, then he should do so.

> **Get your dog to start thinking and responding better to commands around the house. It will pay off with qualifying scores in the end, both in the obedience and in the agility rings.**

Chapter 4

Some Things Old

Do you remember the first time you attended a basic obedience class with your dog? Your instructor probably emphasized how important the commands "sit," "down," "stay," and "come" were if you wanted to own a well-mannered dog. Today if you attend a basic agility class, your instructor will probably tell you that those same four commands are necessary if you want to own a dog that will do well in agility.

If you do not have any agility equipment, you can still work with your dog on the following exercises, which you will need to perfect at some point in your training. Before you begin any training, you may want to review the Understanding Lures and Rewards section in Chapter 3.

In agility, you never use a slip or training collar when you are running your dog over jumps or contact obstacles and through tunnels. However, if you are working on obedience exercises, you may use whatever type of collar you choose. Just be sure that if you are training with a slip or prong collar, you change it for a buckle collar before working with any agility equipment.

The commands "sit," "down," and "stay" are needed for the pause table. Reviewing them now will save you time when you introduce your dog to that obstacle. Exhibitors making the transition from obedience to agility are amazed to see how many dogs incur faults at the pause table, the easiest obstacle on the course. This happens not because a dog refuses to get on the table but because it will not assume the "sit" or the "down" or remain on the table. If you compete in AKC or UKC competition, you will need your dog to respond to the command "sit" in addition to the command "down" on the pause table. All the other agility organizations require only a "down-on-the-table." Because AKC offers the most agility trials, you are likely to compete in these trials and therefore encounter a "sit" on the table. Not only must your dog sit on command, he also needs to learn to sit up from the "down." Why is that? In case he lies down on the table first, then you will have to get him back into a sitting position. When a dog refuses to respond to the "sit" or "down," many exhibitors call their dogs off the table. They then retry a second or even a third time to get their dogs up on the table in the right position. At the higher levels of agility, you probably will not make time if this is what you have to do.

Goal: To Review or Teach the "Sit"

By the time you read this book, your dog should know the command "sit." If he does not, teach the "sit" by using the following steps.

Step 1

Hold a lure in your right hand and place your left hand in your dog's collar. As you say, "Sit," raise the lure above his head. If necessary, gently pull up and back on his collar to get him to sit. As soon as he responds, reward him with his motivator and praise. Release him from the "sit" with a "release word." I use the same word as I do for releasing my dogs from the contact obstacles. I use a very scientific word: "OK"!

Repeat the "sit" a number of times. Make him sit for longer periods before releasing him. Notice if he is sitting so quickly that you do not have to put pressure on his collar. Once this is the case, snap a leash onto his collar and repeat the "sit" command. Use the lure and put pressure on the collar by pulling up and back on the leash if necessary. When your dog sits on command every time with slack in the leash, move to Step 2.

Step 2

Hide the motivator. The reward must immediately follow the dog's response to the command. Tell him to sit, but do nothing. If he sits, reward him with his motivator and praise. If he does not sit, pull up and back on the leash. Praise him for sitting, and give him the motivator. When he sits on command every time without you having to use the leash, move him to a schedule of "random reinforcement." A random reinforcement keeps the dog guessing. He knows he will get his motivator, but he is never sure when. The reason some dogs fall apart in the ring is they expect, and receive, reinforcement every time they respond to a command in training. Then, when the reinforcement is not forthcoming in the ring, they quit working.

The "Sit" Correction

My favorite correction for a dog that does not sit is to tap him lightly on his rump, using a few fingers of one hand. I repeat the command quite firmly and sharply as I tap my dog. Your hand is easy to control. If you see your dog start to sit as you move your hand down toward his rump, you can always stop before you touch him. Tapping your dog on the rear gets the point across quickly. The degree of force you use is easily reduced or escalated depending on his reaction. As soon as he is sitting, reward him with his motivator and praise. You want to take his mind off the correction.

Step 3

Obedience dogs are used to working on the left. Start making your dog sit when he is in front of you and on your right. There are going to be times when he will have to sit on the table when he is on your right, or even when he is approaching you from a distance.

Step 4

When your dog is sitting on command every time, start having him sit when he is at a distance from you. You should also practice the "sit" when he is in motion. Tell him, "Sit" when he is five feet away from you, and move in to tap his rear if he does not respond. Start moving backward so he is trotting toward you. Tell him, "Sit" while he is moving. Use your leash to stop his forward motion by raising your hand and tightening the collar. Use your other hand to tap him into the "sit" if necessary. This is similar to the obedience "drop-on-recall" exercise except that you want your dog to sit instead of drop.

Goal: To Review or Teach the "Drop"

In agility, the "down-on-the-table" is equally as important as the "down" command on the "drop-on-recall" in obedience. Your dog's response to "down" means the difference between a qualifying and nonqualifying score in both events. Dominant dogs do not like to "down," or if they do respond to the command, they do it in their own time. The perfect drop occurs when the dog "downs" without sitting first.

> **In agility, your dog will lose precious seconds if he sits before he lies down on the pause table.**

Step 1

You should always "down" your dog from a standing position. Hold his collar in your left hand and a lure in your right hand, at his eye level. Position your hand in his collar so that it is on the right side of his neck. As you say, "Down" (or your command of choice), lower the lure to the ground between his front legs. At the same time, apply slight pressure to his collar in the direction of the floor. When you apply pressure to his neck in the direction of the ground, your dog is less likely to sit first. The moment his body touches the floor, reward him with his motivator and praise.

For the moment, all you are asking him to do is assume the "down" position without first sitting. You are not asking him to stay there. Repeat the "down" a number of times.

> **Most dogs take longer to learn the "down" than they do the "sit."**

After a number of repetitions, no longer permit your dog to get up once you have given him the motivator. With your hand in his collar, keep him in the "down" position for longer periods of time. Release him from the "down" with your release word. Snap on a leash and pull downward on the leash instead of holding the collar when you work on the "down."

Step 2

When you no longer have to put any pressure on the leash and your dog is lying down without first sitting, it is time to move from lure to reward. Hide the motivator. Place your left hand through your dog's collar and give him the command to "down." Do not pretend you are holding a lure by using a hand signal. Your dog is going to have to respond to your verbal command alone. If he does not respond, apply pressure downward on his collar. The moment he reaches the ground, reward him with his motivator and praise. Do not ask him to stay in the "down" position. Give him your release word and let him get up. Repeat this several times until you find you are no longer applying any pressure to his collar. Then start asking him to stay down for longer periods. Move to a schedule of random reinforcement.

The "Down" Correction

Unlike the "sit," you need to understand why your dog is not going down. Is it because he does not understand what you want, or is it a question of dominance? Do not forget you must eventually move from lure to reward. If you feel your dog does not understand what you want, continue using the lure. If you think your dog understands but is choosing not to comply, a correction becomes necessary. Remember that you only use as much force as is necessary to get the job done. Begin by putting your left hand through your dog's collar. If he does not move when you give the command "down," use more force on the collar than you have used in the past. Repeat the "down" command firmly and sharply. The moment he reaches the ground, reward him with his motivator and praise. Repeat. Did you have to correct him the next time, or did you see improvement?

> **Dropping should be instinctive. A fast response to the command "down" might one day save your dog's life.**

If your dog is still not catching on to the "down" command, you may have to move to a stronger correction. For many years, I have used a tap on top of my dog's head if he does not drop when told. Notice I said *tap* and not *bop*. Use a few fingers to tap him on his head, as you tapped his rear on the "sit." Stop your hand from making contact if your dog starts to drop as he sees the correction coming. When you use your hand in this manner, it eventually becomes the "down" hand signal. The moment your dog is lying down, bring out the motivator and reward him to get his mind off the correction. Repeat. You should not have to make that correction many times for him to understand what you want. However, if you are dealing with a dominance issue, you may have to use corrections over a longer period of time. In agility, unlike obedience, you may use both a voice signal and a hand signal to "down" your dog on the pause table.

Step 3

Once you have a reliable drop at your left side, then work on having your dog drop right in front of you and on your right. Start moving backward and drop your dog while he is moving toward you. Then have him drop while he is moving beside you. A dog trained for a CDX title should have learned this long ago.

Step 4

When your dog is dropping every time, try turning the "down" into a game. If you make it fun for him, he is likely to drop faster. Ask him if he is ready, start to crouch, and then tell him to "down" and go into a squat yourself. When he is down, toss him the motivator as you tell him, "Get it," and encourage him to leap up and catch the food or toy.

Goal: To Review or Teach the "Sit from the Down"

I have found the "sit from the down" is one of the most difficult things to perfect in obedience. However, in the obedience ring you do the "sit from the down" at a distance of forty feet. It is much easier to get the dog to do the "sit from the down" when he is close to you. If your dog is trained for utility in obedience, he should already know how to do this. If you have not taught him this exercise, these are the steps to take.

Step 1

Put your dog on leash. Have him lie down on your left side, and then turn sideways toward him. Hold your motivator in your right hand in front of his nose. Tell him to sit, and raise the motivator above and a little behind his head. Apply tension to the leash with your left hand; this will help him sit up. Reward him with his motivator and praise. Repeat until he is popping up into the "sit" without any tension on his collar.

Step 2

Hide the motivator. Turn sideways toward your dog with your legs spread about eighteen inches apart, your right leg placed in front of your left. Your feet should be facing his legs. When you tell him to sit, swing the inside of your right foot close to the ground toward his paws. Brush his paws with your foot if necessary, and at the same time, pull back on his collar with the leash. When he pops up into a "sit," reward him with his motivator and praise.

The "Sit from the Down" Correction

The correction for the "sit from the down" is actually to bump the front of your dog's feet with the inside of your right foot as you swing your leg toward him.

Step 3

Practice by having him "sit from the down" when he is in front of you and when he is lying on your right. Turn the "sit" into a game. Have him lie down. Ask him, "Are you ready?" and then give him the "sit" command. As soon as he sits, toss the motivator to him, giving a "get it" command, and have him leap up to catch his reward.

Goal: To Review the "Stay"

There are two places where you need a solid "stay" on an agility course. One is on the pause table. The other is at the start line, unless you have a dog with which you do not have to "lead out." (See Chapter 2, Agility Jargon section.) Many owners of the smaller or slower breeds do not find it necessary to lead out with their dogs. The clock does not start running until your dog, not you, crosses the start line. This can be a problem if you lead out and your dog breaks the "stay." You may not be in the right position to call him when he starts the clock. He may actually miss the first obstacles on the course if you are not where you had planned to stand when he jumped the gun. A dog starting before the handler is ready has ruined many a run. This is one more reason why a solid "stay" is so important in this sport.

> There are many dogs showing in obedience that do not have a solid "stay." There are equally as many in the agility ring!

Have you ever left your dog on a "sit stay" or "down stay" on leash and then gone too far, whereby the leash has tightened and your dog has gotten up? Bet you said something like, "Sorry, my fault!" If your dog truly understood the command "stay," he would not have budged! Many trainers do not put their dogs to the test, to see if they understand what "stay" really means. If your dog never breaks a stay, what does it tell you? Is it because your dog understands the exercise, or are you just lucky?

Step 1

With your dog on leash, have him sit. Tell him to stay and walk away, applying light tension to the leash as you go. Does he stay? If he does, then turn to face him, and apply tension again. Gradually increase the tension until you can pull quite hard and he still stays there. (See Figure 4-1.) What happens if he gets up as soon as he feels tension on his collar? First, remember you have just been using pressure on the collar to make him "sit" and "down," so it might be understandable if he should get confused and think you want him to move. If he starts to get up, immediately let him know he is wrong. You can say something like "boo-boo," "wrong," "no," or "uh-uh." Use whatever words you say to give him information that he made a mistake. Place him back where he

Figure 4-1. Tension on the leash on a "sit stay."

had been sitting, and start over. Most dogs catch on to this game quickly. If he stays, you should return to him and reward him for staying. Toss him the motivator, have a game of tag, and let him know how well he has done. It is impossible to lure a dog into staying.

Step 2

When he is solid at staying in the "sit" with tension on the leash, then do the same thing with the "down stay." Put tension on the leash as you walk away from your dog and when you are at a distance in front of him. Finally, with him lying beside you, apply upward tension on the leash to see if he understands to remain in the "down" position. (See Figure 4-2.) Unlike in obedience, if your dog sits up from the "down" on the pause table during the count, he can still pass. The judge starts the count over once you have your dog lying back down again. All you lose are precious seconds, which could cost you dearly with time faults at the advanced level.

Figure 4-2. Testing your dog's understanding of "down"
*by applying tension **up** on the leash.*

Step 3

When your dog is at the start line or on the pause table, he probably is anxiously waiting for you to call him. A slight movement on your part might be all it takes to make him get up. Teach him to stay in place no matter what you do. When he is on a "sit stay" or "down stay," stand at a distance from him and suddenly leap sideways. He will probably get up to join you. Put him back and try again. In the beginning when you do this, you might want to say, "Stay" as you move, to remind him what he is supposed to be doing. When he understands what you want, then take off running. He should hold position.

Goal: To Review the "Come"

One might expect every dog starting out in agility to have a reliable "come" command. That is not always the case. Many exhibitors have a "ring come" but not a "come-under-all-circumstances come." (See Chapter 3, the section called How Well Does Your Dog Listen at Home?) A favorite saying of the late dog trainer Jack Godsil was that a dog was not completely trained unless you could turn him loose in a parking lot and know he would come when you called him. Now I do not know of anyone who would be stupid enough to put that to the test, but I am sure you get the point he was trying to make.

I expect my own dogs to have a reliable recall by the time they are four months old. When I am working with a young dog, I always have treats or a toy in my pocket. When I call my dog, he is always rewarded, indoors and out. This is one time when I do not move to a schedule of random reinforcement right away. I really want my dog to want to come to me. I also do a lot of work on a twenty-six-foot retractable leash. I take my puppy/dog out to many different places, and when he gets distracted, that is when I call him. I pop the retractable leash if I do not get an immediate response to my call. If I do not see the results I want, my dog wears a check cord around the house. This way I can always catch him if he chooses to ignore me. My check cord is an eight-foot piece of heavy nylon twist cord with a snap at one end and no handle at the other. I want the cord to drag freely. If I call my dog and get no response, I always go and get him. Many dogs try to split as soon as they see you approaching. This is where the check cord comes in handy. Unless your dog is very fast, you can always step on the cord and snag him. Pick the cord up and make a correction. My correction is a few pops on the leash as I say, sharply and firmly, "Come" several times over. When the pup reaches me, I produce the motivator and we have a game. I want my dog to want to come to me, and he must understand that there is no option in this case.

Step 1

When you have a solid "stay," you can leave your dog and then call him to you. You do not need to have your dog "front" as you might in obedience. Begin with your dog on leash. When he reaches you, reward him with his motivator and praise. Call him to you from both the "sit" and the "down." When he is on the pause table, he will need to come to you or go to the next obstacle from either a "down" or "sit."

Step 2

Practice off leash. Call him to you from various distances and angles. There is seldom such a thing as a straight-on recall in agility.

Chapter 5

Some Things New

In obedience, you do not always have to set up an open or utility ring when you train. You might just work on "fronts" and "stays" or the dumbbell and signals in limited space. We call this *"hearth rug training."* The exercises in this chapter fall into this category. You do not need any agility equipment to practice these exercises. Eventually, when you have equipment to set up, you can concentrate on the things that need more space.

There are times on an agility course where you might find yourself ahead of your dog and you need to have him catch up to you on one side or the other. He will also have to run on your right, as well as your left, for a considerable distance. The sooner you get him to feel comfortable being on your right, the better.

Teaching Your Dog to Work on Your Right

You do not want your dog to give you the type of attentive heel work that you expect in the obedience ring. When you run with your dog on your heel side, you may want to use a different command. You could say, "Let's go." My dogs are so *context-oriented* (see Chapter 3) that I find my regular "heel" command works just fine in agility. However, I do not get the same type of attentive heeling that I usually do in the obedience ring. My dogs seem to know that there is a difference by the way I am moving.

Goal: To Teach Your Dog to Move on Your Right Side

Step 1

Show your dog his motivator. Leave your dog on an on-leash "sit stay." With the leash in your right hand, walk forward until it tightens slightly. If you have taught "tension on the leash," your dog should remain sitting. Pause, with your back to your dog. Pass the leash over to your left hand so that it crosses in front of your body. Hold your motivator in your right hand and extend your right arm away from your side with your palm toward your dog. Tell your dog, "Side," and start moving forward. Encourage "Sport" to catch up to your right side. Reward him by allowing him to take his motivator out of your hand and praise him. Repeat this several times, and then duplicate the exercise by having him come up to you on the "heel" side.

Step 2

When your dog appears to understand that he is to come up on your right, start moving forward and have him run with you several steps before you allow him to take his motivator. Many dogs trained in obedience find running on the right hard to do. Their rears swing out, and they have difficulty moving in a straight line. They even tend to swing around in front of you and start moving backward. You may have had a similar experience when you first taught your dog to "heel" in obedience. The name for this action is "crabbing out." You probably fixed it on heeling, but there will be no carryover when your dog is moving on your right. If you have this problem, do not begin the exercise with your dog catching up to your right side. Instead, start with him sitting beside you on your right. "Double-leash" him for a few sessions: Have him wear two collars. Hold one leash in your right hand, and pass the other leash behind your back and hold it in your left hand. As your dog's rear starts to swing to his right, tighten the leash that you are holding in your left hand. When his rear moves back in line, add slack to the leash. You are not concerned with teaching your dog to "heel" on your right. You simply want to teach him to stay on your right and move in a straight line.

Step 3

Once your dog can move in a straight line beside you on your right side, alternate between calling him to your right and left sides, off leash. Have him catch up to you from farther away. Have him run beside you on your right for a greater distance before you give him his motivator.

Step 4

Teach your dog to move to your right side from his "heel" side. Walk away from him and put your left hand out to your side. However, hold your motivator in your right hand close to your body. Call your dog to come to your "heel" side. As he is about to catch up to you, place your left arm at your side and say, "Side" and extend your right arm away from your body. He should then change direction and come up on your right side. Reward him with his motivator and praise him. Repeat this several times. Occasionally, do this in reverse. Hold the motivator in your left hand and call him to your right side. Switch him over to your left, as he is about to catch up to you. Be sure that you switch the side you want him to be on before he has reached you.

"Leave It"

Goal: To Teach Your Dog the Command "Leave It"

You may have already taught this command in obedience. In agility, you are bound to be doing some targeting. If, for some reason, you do not want your dog to get the target, then you will need a command to have him leave the target where it is. It is always possible that your dog will decide to cheat. What is meant by cheating is that he might run to the target, bypassing several obstacles. You do not want to reward him for cheating, so you need to be able to call him off the target. When you teach "leave it," you can use food, a toy, or a combination of the two.

"Leave it" is a useful command for any dog to learn, regardless
of whether he is an agility dog, a hunting dog, an obedience
dog, or a family pet.

Step 1

Place a piece of food between the tips of the fingers and thumb of one
hand and hold your hand so the palm is facing you. When your dog
comes over to sniff your hand and try to grab the food, tell him, "Leave
it." At the same time, flip the back of your hand toward him so that your
knuckles rap him lightly on his nose. He should be taken by surprise,
but only momentarily. He will almost certainly try to reach for the food
again. Repeat the same procedure. Most dogs when treated in this way
will stand there, wondering what you are up to. When he has ignored
whatever you have in your hand for several seconds, praise him and
then tell him, "OK, get it," and offer him the treat. Continue to do this
until, when he starts to sniff your hand and you tell him to leave it, he
will move his head away from your hand. Praise him, and then give him
a treat with the command to get it.

Step 2

Put your dog on leash. Toss a toy or piece of food a few feet out in
front of you and tell your dog, "Get it." Repeat this several times. Then,
toss out the food or toy but say nothing. If your dog starts to go after
the object say, "Leave it." If necessary, tighten the leash. When he stops
and looks at you, praise him, and then give him your release command
and tell him to get it. Practice this until he immediately stops going after
the toy or food whenever you say, "Leave it."

Step 3

Try the same thing off leash. If he ignores you and grabs the food, you
will have to put him back on leash. If he is smart enough to go after the

food only when the leash is off, then use a food tube instead. Instructions for making a food tube can be found in Appendix B, or you can order one from *Clean Run* (see Appendix A). If he grabs the toy, take it away from him and say something like, "Hey, I said leave it!"

Step 4

Throw out the toy or food about fifteen to twenty feet and tell him, "Get it." As he gets about halfway to the object, tell him, "Leave it" and call him back to you. Praise him and release him to get the object. Practicing this exercise will help with call-offs later on.

"Through"

Goal: To Teach Your Dog to Run Through Your Legs

Before I ever considered making the transition to agility, I taught my dogs to run through my legs on the recall. I did this to make them focus on the center of my body and, also, to speed up the recall. I used the command "through." I started the game by sitting my dog a few feet in front of me, while I dangled a toy in front of my legs. I told my dog, "Get it" and tossed the toy through my legs as he reached the "front" position. Later, I held the same toy behind my back and tossed it out from behind. My dogs quickly caught on to this game, and once they did, I added the word "through." If I called them on the recall with the command "through," they would race toward me and run through my legs without an additional command. I never dreamed how easily this would transfer to teaching the tunnel. My dogs understood "through" to mean run through something. They mastered the tunnel the first time they saw one.

"Get Out"

Obstacles on agility courses are often positioned off to the side of the path you and your dog are traveling. Because of the layout of the course, you may not always be able to run with your dog all the way to an obstacle. Faced with this situation, you need to use a command that tells your dog to move laterally away from you to reach the next obstacle in the sequence. The command most commonly used in agility is "get out" or "out." This command can be introduced without the use of any agility equipment and, more importantly, can be taught in a confined space.

I have found it easiest to teach a dog to "get out" to a large traffic cone. I do not recommend using a small cone because these cones are often used to number the obstacles at a trial. Should you use a small cone for this exercise, your dog might become confused about what he is supposed to do when presented with many small cones on an agility course.

Goal: To Introduce the "Get Out" Command

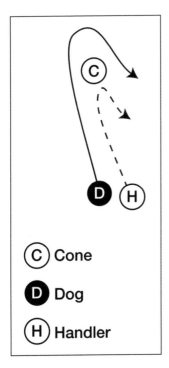

(C) Cone

(D) Dog

(H) Handler

Figure 5-1A.
The "get out" command.

Step 1

To your left, place a large cone, bucket, or jump upright about three feet away and at a 45-degree angle to where you are standing. Have your dog on your left. Hold a motivator in your left hand. You will be using the motivator as a lure. Tell your dog, "Get out," and signal toward the cone with your left hand while, at the same time, moving toward it. Have your dog follow your hand around the cone, moving clockwise from left to right. Your arm will be above the top of the cone. As soon as he passes around the back of the cone and moves toward you, allow him to have his motivator, and praise. (See Figure 5-1A.) Repeat this several times, and then start over with the cone and your dog on your right. You will hold your motivator in your right hand, and your dog will move around the cone counterclockwise from right to left.

Step 2

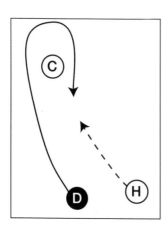

Set the exercise up as before. This time hide the motivator in your right hand. You will be using the motivator as a reward. Tell your dog, "Get out," and signal toward the cone with your left hand. At the same time, step toward the cone, but do not go all the way to it. (See Figure 5-1B.) If your dog runs around the cone without the use of a lure, give him the motivator out of your right hand, and praise. If he stops when you stop, you can do one of two things. Either do more repetitions using the lure, or take him by his collar and lead him around the cone, giv-

Figure 5-1B.

ing him an additional command to "get out" using a firm voice. Once he is reliably running around the cone on the left without assistance, repeat the exercise with the cone on the right. He may find this more difficult to do. Remember that your dog is probably not as confident working off your right.

Step 3

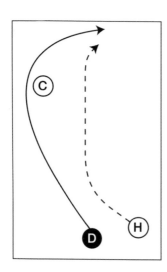

When your dog is reliably running around the cones on both sides, it is time to increase the distance you send him on his "get out." When you taught your dog the "go out" in obedience, you only increased the distance you sent him by a foot at a time. This is also the case with the "get out." As you send your dog, always take at least one step in the direction you want him to go, but do not go all the way to the cone. Instead, as he is running toward the cone, start moving forward, parallel to the cone. (See Figure 5-1C.) After your dog has run around the cone, call him to you, or toss him his motivator.

Figure 5-1C.

Step 4

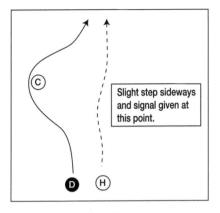

Slight step sideways and signal given at this point.

Figure 5-2.
"Get out" while dog and handler are moving forward together.

Your dog will need to "get out" when he is moving next to you on an agility course, so you need to teach him the "get out" in motion. Place the cone about three feet to the side of your line of travel. Move forward with your dog on the left side. When you are about ten feet away from the cone, tell your dog, "Get out," and step sideways in the direction of the cone. (See Figure 5-2.) At the same time, give your signal. If he takes off running around the cone, be ready to toss him his motivator as he comes around the cone. If he does not leave you, take him by the collar and lead him around the cone. He may need to do more repetitions from a stationary position. Once he understands what you are asking, move the cone to your right side and send him when he is moving beside you on your right.

Step 5

Increase the distance your dog will "get out" when you are moving with him at your side. Once your dog understands what is required by this exercise, the "get out" to obstacles will be easy for him.

Switching Sides

During a novice agility course, you may only have to make one change of side. A change of side is necessary when the course changes direction. You may begin running the course with your dog on your left, and at some point you may need to have him run on your right. At the novice level, a change of sides is likely to occur when the dog is on the pause table, in a contact zone, or in a tunnel. These would be termed static or blind crosses. (See Chapter 2.) At the more advanced levels, you will be changing sides several times during the course, often when both you and your dog are moving. A dynamic side switch is probably the most difficult maneuver for your dog to master in agility, and the timing of it is critical. If you have a slow dog and you can run alongside him, you may never need a "cross behind." You should always be able to cross in front of him.

You can teach a "cross behind" without the use of any equipment. Your dog will find this exercise easier to learn when he is moving slowly and can concentrate on only one thing. A "cross behind" may be a difficult concept for your dog to grasp. He is not used to having you suddenly move to his opposite side when you are both moving forward together. In obedience, that would be considered a no-no.

What constitutes a "cross behind"? A "cross behind" occurs when YOU cross your dog's path at some point on the course, when he is moving ahead of you. You are not crossing behind an obstacle; instead you are crossing behind your dog's path. Your dog will then move in a new direction based on your change in position.

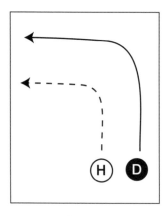

Figure 5-3.

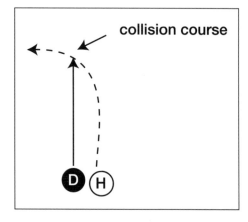

Figure 5-4. There is a potential for collision
when your dog is on your left and you turn left.

If you need to turn your dog to the left, you will find it simple to do if he is running on your right. As you turn left, you will pull him in the new direction. (See Figure 5-3.) However, it is difficult to turn him to the left when he is running next to you, on your left, without the two of you colliding. (See Figure 5-4.) If your dog is ahead of you, you can cross behind his path so that he will then be on your right. You can then turn left, call your dog, and escape from having a collision. (See Figure 5-5.)

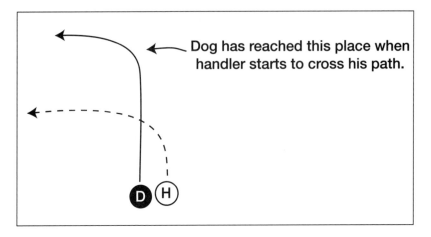

Dog has reached this place when handler starts to cross his path.

Figure 5-5. Turning left by crossing your dog's path when he is out ahead of you.

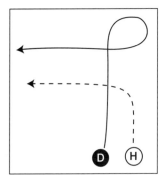

Figure 5-6. Dog turns in the wrong direction and has to spin.

Dogs remember which side their handlers are on. Obedience-trained dogs will likely turn in toward their handlers when they are called. If you start running with your dog on your left, and you tell him, "Come," he will most likely turn to his right toward where he expects you to be. However, if you crossed behind him moments earlier and he did not notice, he would probably still turn to the right. He should turn left instead. If he turned right, then in order to catch up to you, he would have to spin (make a 270-degree turn), which costs time. (See Figure 5-6.) What you really want to happen is to have your dog recognize your change of side from right to left and turn left. This takes a lot of practice.

Did you ever teach your dog a "come front" exercise? Most obedience dogs learned this when being trained on "fronts" for the recall. You would "heel" with your dog and then suddenly stop and begin to back up. Your dog would turn in toward you and come to a "front" position. This exercise is ingrained in many obedience dogs. For this reason, the "cross behind" can cause problems until the dog understands what to do.

Before I taught the "cross behind" away from agility equipment, I had many problems with an old, highly competitive obedience dog not grasping the idea of the cross. I got a lot of spinning and time faults. Nothing anyone suggested worked, but all the suggestions I received recommended teaching the "cross behind" while using the jumps. Finally, I decided to try to teach her the "cross behind" as an obedience exercise, and it worked well. I have used this concept with every dog I have trained since that time.

Goal: To Introduce Your Dog to a Change of Side

Step 1

With your dog wearing a leash, put your dog on a "stand stay." Your dog should be wearing a buckle collar. Stand in "heel" position, holding the leash in your left hand, with the leash positioned so that it runs from under your dog's chin along the left side of your dog's body. Slowly back up until you are about one foot behind the dog's rear end. You will notice that your dog's head will turn to his right as you do this, and his body is likely to start leaning to the right also. Step sideways to position yourself on your dog's left. As you do so, reach forward and grasp the leash with your right hand. Tell your dog, "Switch," or "Cross." At the same time, pull gently on the leash toward you and make a 90-degree turn to your left. Say, "Side," and move forward quickly. You will discover that your dog may try to turn to the right. As long as you have tension on the leash, you should be able to prevent this from happening. Reward him if he turns in the correct direction. Repeat several times in this one direction until he is making no mistakes. It will be obvious when he understands what you want. With your dog on your left as you start to back up, his head will start to turn to the right. When you step to your left, you will see his head suddenly snap to the left before he starts to move. Repeat this exercise with your dog standing on your right, and step to the right behind him. He should turn his head to the right before turning to catch up to you.

Step 2

Once your dog is turning correctly in each direction, step back two feet beyond his rear end and then three feet. Practice until you can stand at the end of a six-foot leash, step sideways, and have him turn the correct way. I have found the greater the distance you step behind your dog, the more likely the dog thinks he is doing a "come front" and the more likely he is to turn the wrong way. He may revert back to turning right when he should be turning left or vice versa. Keep practicing until he seldom makes a mistake.

Step 3

I also make a game out of this exercise. I have my dog stand, and then I step back until I can move easily behind him. Then I step one way but do not say anything. As his head turns in the direction I am moving, I quickly step back the other way and then back the opposite way again. I just give my praise word as my dog turns his head in the correct direction. I want him to understand that I want him to just turn his head and do nothing else. All my dogs seem to enjoy this game.

Goal: To "Cross Behind" While Moving

Step 1

You next progress to working on this when both you and your dog are moving. The placement of your hands on the leash is important for the success of this step. With your dog on your left, hold the leash in both hands with your right hand in front of your left, slightly closer to your dog's collar. Be sure to position the leash to the left of his body. Tell him, "Let's go" and move out slowly, encouraging your dog to move out ahead of you just a little. After walking forward several steps, tell him, "Stay" or "Wait." The moment he hesitates, cross behind him to his other side. As you do so, say, "Switch" or "Cross," and then turn to the left and continue walking. It does not matter if your dog stands or sits when he hesitates. Once you have crossed behind your dog, he should turn to the left and catch up with you on your right side. Reward him. Repeat several times in the same direction only. Then start over with your dog on your right. Hold the leash with your left hand in front of your right. This time you will have your dog turn to the right.

If your dog wants to turn in the wrong direction, you may need to do the following. Hold the leash in the hand nearest your dog. As you start to cross behind him, place the palm of your other hand against his face and push his head in the direction you are moving. For example, if your dog is on your left, hold the leash in your left hand. As you step to the left, place the palm of your right hand on the right side of his face, and push his head to his left. This is not done as a correction, merely to assist him in turning in the proper direction.

Step 2

The next step is to stop saying "stay" or "wait" as you start to cross behind your dog. Simply say, "Cross" or "Switch," move behind your dog, and then turn 90-degrees and start walking in the new direction. When he has no trouble turning in one direction, repeat in the other. Finally, after you have completed the "cross behind," switch the placement of your hands on the leash so that you can repeat the "cross behind" in the opposite direction.

You will find it helpful in the beginning if you do the following leash handling. As you move from the right side of the dog to the left, move your right hand both to the right and forward, moving your dog slightly out to his right. Then move your right hand to the left as you bring your dog to your right side. Do the reverse when practicing having your dog turn to the right. Remember, you are not working on a slip collar, and you are not making corrections.

Should your dog turn in the wrong direction, say, "Ah, ah" or whatever expression you use to let your dog know he did the wrong thing, and repeat the exercise. If necessary, go back a step and have your dog pause while you make the cross so he has time to think about what you are doing.

Eventually, you should be able to take a walk with your dog on leash and cross back and forth behind him without even making a 90-degree turn. He should continue to walk in a relatively straight line, just glancing over his shoulder to see where you are going.

I practice this crossing back and forth, without jumps, as one of my warm-up exercises at a trial.

Chapter 6

Some Things Borrowed

If a dog you have trained has earned his AKC or UKC UD title, then you have probably been exposed to some form of targeting. For years obedience trainers have used targeting for teaching the "go outs."

In agility, you want your dog to work ahead of you if possible. How do you teach your dog to do that? Obedience dogs tend to want to stay close to their handlers. One of the best ways is to teach your dog to run to a target. Your target can be food, a toy, or even a touch stick. There is no set rule about what type of target to use. The best target is something the dog really wants. It is a good idea to teach your dog targeting before introducing him to the agility equipment. Targeting is hearth rug training.

If you are going to use food for a target, you should consider one thing right from the beginning. If the food target is placed right on the ground, you may end up with a dog with a sniffing problem. In obedience, you can always recognize a trainer who has placed food on the floor at the end of the ring to teach the "go out." The trainer's dog runs out on the send away, drops his head, and starts sniffing the ground. If I am using food, I like to place it up off the ground so that it is visible to the dog. The exceptions to this rule in agility are on the contact obstacles and the table. Other than on the contacts and table, the food target should be easily reached without the dog having to drop his head and large enough for the dog to see easily. You do not want your dog searching for his tidbit. This encourages sniffing. There are as many sniffing problems to be seen in the agility ring as the obedience ring.

Goal: To Teach Your Dog to Go to a Target

Step 1

Put your dog on a "sit stay," and then walk out and place your target about six feet in front of him. A toy can be placed on the ground, but put food on an inverted bucket or on top of a plastic food container. Tell your dog, "Look" as you do so. Return to him so that you are standing with him on your left. Restrain him by the collar and then tell him, "Look" once more. Next, give him his release word, tell him, "Get it," and let go of the collar. Praise him as he runs towards the target. If you only send him a short distance in the beginning, you will be guaranteed success. Repeat this several times.

Step 2

Switch to having him run to the target from your right. After several repetitions, increase the distance you are sending him to the target from both your right and left sides. When you feel certain that he is catching on to this game, no longer tell him, "Look" when you place the target out. However, continue to tell him, "Look" when you are at his side. Restrain him by holding his collar and do not send him for the target until he is looking in the right direction.

Step 3

Once your dog is running about ten feet to the target, it is time to introduce a command that means "go ahead of me." It would be wise not to use your "go out" command from utility. If I were sending my dog out ahead of me to a target I would say, "Look. (pause) Go. (pause) OK, get it." The command "look" would be used to get my dog to look ahead, and "go" is his command to run ahead of me. (I use "away" for my utility "go out" command.) "OK, get it" is given just before he reaches the target so he knows it is OK to take the food or toy.

As I increase the distance to the target, I continue to restrain my dog. I want him to get used to "flying out of the box," so to speak. Remember that agility is run against the clock. When you restrain your dog, he is more likely to take off fast once you release him, particularly if, as you restrain him, you start whispering, "Are you ready? Are you going to get it?" or something like that. You want to psyche him up to take off quickly.

Eventually you will need to be able to call him off the target with your "leave it" command. You should not do this very often, but you must have this tool in your training box of tricks. As mentioned earlier, the reason you might need to call your dog off the target is because you may be working him over a series of obstacles when he decides to cheat.

Step 4

Tell him, "Look," "Go," and then "Leave it," and call him back to you. When he reaches you, praise him and then release him to go back to the target.

When you train in agility, it is preferable to have a training partner with whom to work. However, this is not always possible. If you train by yourself, and you have a dog that is likely to cheat, you should use a food tube if you use an edible target. This way, once your dog reaches the target, he will only be rewarded if you give him the food. If he cheats, he will be unable to reward himself. If your dog cheats when you use a toy as your target, you can always take the toy away. It would be preferable that he did not get the toy, but if you use food and do not use a food tube, you will certainly not be able to remove the food from his stomach. Instructions for making or buying a food tube are to be found in Appendix B.

Chapter 7

Win the Blue

The significance of blue in agility is the same as in obedience. It means first place. In agility, the first place winner of each height division wins a blue ribbon. If you own one of the non-obedience-oriented breeds, you will find it is easier to win a blue ribbon and earn a perfect score in agility than it is in obedience.

Chapter 8

Getting over
the First Hurdle

Obstacle commands for the jumps are usually "jump," "over," "hup," "big jump," or "big over."

Agility courses will consist of more single bar jumps than any other kind of jump. A single bar jump is a jump with two bars. Do not confuse a single bar jump with a jump that has only one bar, which is called a one-bar jump. With only one bar, this jump is more difficult for your dog to see, and it is also easier for him to run under. Your dog will also have to learn to jump spread jumps, which are comprised of a broad jump, a double bar jump, and a triple bar jump. There is also a tire jump and a panel jump. The panel jump is an obedience high jump with displaceable boards. When you start your jump training, you will be using single bar jumps if you have made some; otherwise make do with your obedience jumps. Single bar jumps are the easiest jumps to move and set up.

Although you may not own much agility equipment, you must practice with your dog just as you would in obedience. You can do quite a lot of jumping in a small space if you only have two or three jumps. The more often you practice, the sooner you will be able to compete. One of the advantages of obedience over agility is that you do not need as much room to practice. Most people can find enough space to practice signals and articles even if they do not have enough room for directed retrieve and directed jumping. To start sequence jumping, you really need a minimum area of 60′ × 20′ for training. If you do not have that much space available, you will need to go to the closest public open space that allows your dog to accompany you and work off leash. This can be a problem for some who do not live in a dog-friendly community. Believe it or not, some dog exhibitors end up moving to another house to have more room for their addiction.

You can use your obedience jump command for agility. Many handlers add the word *big* for the spread jumps. Personally, I do not see that it makes any difference to a dog's performance, but there certainly is nothing wrong with using a different command for a spread jump if you wish.

Because the majority of obedience dogs are most comfortable working on the handler's left, every time you introduce your dog to something new in agility, begin the exercise with your dog on your left, his comfort zone. However, as soon as your dog has grasped the concept of what you are trying to convey, you should immediately start working the dog on your right. You should also do two or three times the number of repetitions with your dog on your right so that he starts to feel comfortable being on that side.

When you set up your jumps always place the jump bars so that each bar is resting with one end on one side of the uprights and the other end on the opposite side. This way if your dog approaches the jump from either direction and displaces a bar, it will fall down without tripping him. Some jumps are made with cups to support the bars between the uprights. With this style of jump, the bars will drop easily when hit from either direction.

Is Your Dog Right- or Left-pawed?

Do you know if your dog is right- or left-pawed? Knowing this will explain why your dog can turn tighter and faster in one direction than in the other. There are several ways to tell which is his dominant side. First, when your dog is running freely ahead of you, call him to "come." Do this a number of times. Notice which way he naturally turns—is it to the right or to the left? Most dogs will turn the same way almost every time. If your dog retrieves, throw out a toy. Your dog will run to pick it up and bring it back to you, most likely turning the same way every time. Put your dog on a "sit stay." Walk off about thirty feet and call him. On which leg does he start? In horse terms, this is called a lead. If your dog favors turning to the left, he will also lead with his left leg. You will find he will also be able to turn more easily to the left than to the right. His body will be more flexible in that direction because he always turns that way. If you have a dog that favors turning to the left, you have a southpaw dog. Most dogs are right-pawed, just as most humans are right-handed. Are south-paw dogs more gifted? My best dogs have all been southpaws!

In obedience, your dog only has to make a sharp turn after a jump during the broad jump exercise, and he only has to turn in one direc-tion. In agility, particularly in the jumpers classes, your dog will be jumping and then turning many times on the course. Because agility is run against the clock, the tighter you can get your dog to turn, the fewer steps he will have to take on the course. The shorter distance your dog has to travel, the faster his run will be. Many dogs will end up out in the back forty if given half a chance, so you should teach your dog how to jump and turn early in training. This training will teach him how to flex his body, something he may not be used to doing.

At agility trials, a warm-up jump is provided for exhibitors to use. Even though there is usually only one jump available, it does give you an opportunity to practice turns and sending your dog over a jump. The following exercises use only one or two jumps and can be practiced in a very small space. In the teaching phase, set up the jumps at a height that will be effortless for your dog.

Control Exercises That Only Use One or Two Jumps

A fast dog will benefit from training with one or two jumps. A fast dog may get out of control if you only work on sequencing. Working a slow dog on one or two jumps may tend to slow the dog down even more and should be kept to a minimum. Obedience exhibitors often polish their dogs by working only on fronts and finishes rather than the entire recall. In agility, you can break down jumping exercises in a sim-ilar manner.

One-Jump Exercises

*Goal: To Teach Your Dog to Jump Over One Jump and
Return Quickly to You*

Step 1

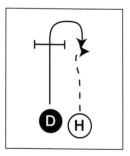

*Figure 8-1. Handler
running with dog on left.*

Start about eight to ten feet from the jump. You are not looking for speed, simply control. Begin with your dog on your left. Hold the leash in your left hand. Tell your dog, "Go jump," and run toward the jump. The moment he is in the air, step to your right and say, "Come." (See Figure 8-1.) This is a similar movement to the "come front" exercise in obedience. The difference is that your dog must first take a jump before he turns toward you. You do not want the dog to return to you over the jump, so be sure to step away from the jump as you call him. When a dog returns over a jump in agility, it is called back jumping. If your dog does this, it is considered a wrong course, which can lead to a penalty or elimination. Unfortunately, in open obedience you have worked on jumping by teaching the dog to take the jump in both directions! This could be confusing for your dog, so you may have to spend extra time working on this new concept. It is quite likely that the leash will tighten if your dog does not make a tight turn when you call him. Keep slack in the leash until after your dog has landed. If the leash tightens while he is in the air, it could throw him off balance, and he might slip as he lands. Reward him. Repeat several times.

Step 2

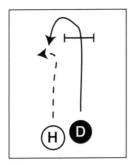

Figure 8-2. Handler running with dog on right.

Start over with your dog on your right. You will hold your leash in your right hand. Your dog will be turning left upon landing, a new concept for him. (See Figure 8-2.) Repeat several times. You may find your dog does not turn as tightly as he does to the right because his body is not used to turning tightly in this direction.

Goal: To Have Your Dog Come Up to Your Left or Right Side After the Turn

Step 1

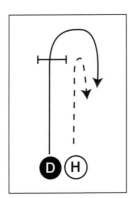

Figure 8-3. Handler turns right and calls dog to left side.

Set up the jump as in the previous exercise. Run with your dog on your left toward the jump. As he is in the air, say, "Come." As he lands, turn 180 degrees to your right, away from the jump. Run back toward your starting point. (See Figure 8-3.) After you turn, switch your leash into your right hand. Hold your left hand out away from your side and encourage your dog to come up to your left side. Reward him with a treat or a toy. You should have already taught him to catch up to your side if you followed the suggestions in Chapter 5. Repeat this several times and then start over with your dog on your right. When you turn to the left, away from the jump, switch your leash to your left hand. Hold your right hand out to encourage your dog to come up on your right side.

Step 2

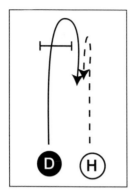

Figure 8-4. Handler turns left and calls dog to handler's right side.

Set up the exercise as before, with your dog on your left. This time when you turn, you will turn in toward the jump and have your dog catch up to your right side. (See Figure 8-4.) As you make the turn, change the leash first to your right hand as you make the turn and then back to your left as you start to run. You need your right hand to be free to signal to your dog to come up on your right side. When you turn in toward the jump, your dog may try to back jump. Be ready to stop him. After he has turned and run by the jump upright successfully several times, repeat with him on your right. You will be turning to your right, and your dog will catch up to your left side. You want your dog to turn as tightly as possible, so keep the leash on for several training sessions. Then try these exercises with your dog off leash. If your dog goes wide on the turns, put the leash back on for several more sessions.

When you no longer have to have your dog on leash, you will be able to incorporate a hand signal to send your dog over the jump. When you begin running with your dog, say, "Go jump." In addition, you will direct your dog toward each obstacle by motioning with whichever arm is closest to the obstacle he is supposed to take. This is a difficult concept for many obedience exhibitors who are used to only using certain arms for specific signals. Most of the time in agility, you do not signal across your body with your hand, unless you wish to turn your dog away from you.

Goal: To Teach Your Dog a Jumping Figure 8 Using One Jump

Many exhibitors practice this exercise at an agility trial when they warm up their dogs.

Step 1

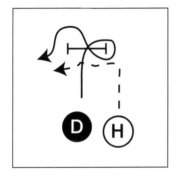

Figure 8-5. Jumping figure 8.

Start with your dog off leash, on your left, about eight feet in front of the jump. Tell him, "Go jump," give a signal with your left arm, and move with him toward the jump. As your dog is in mid-air, say, "Come," and start to back up quickly. As your dog starts to come around the right jump upright toward you, move laterally to the left. Step toward the jump, giving a signal with your right arm and say, "Go jump." Your dog should turn to his right and take the jump diagonally, a second time. Continue to move to your left. As your dog is in the air, say, "Come," and call him to you around the left jump upright. (See Figure 8-5.) Reward. Repeat this exercise, starting with your dog on your right. This time, when you call him after he has taken the jump, you will move laterally to your right and then step forward and send your dog diagonally over the jump for the second time from your left side.

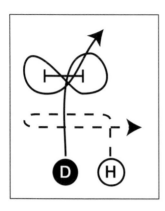

Figure 8-6.

Step 2

Start as in the previous exercise. This time, after your dog takes the jump for the second time, call him back around the left upright and then step forward, signal with your left arm toward the jump, and send him over a third time. (See Figure 8-6.) He will be taking the jump first from your left side, then from your right, and then from your left again. Repeat the exercise with your dog starting on your right. This exercise looks like the obedience figure 8 with the jump uprights taking the place of the stewards.

Two-Jump Exercises

Goal: To Have Your Dog Jump Two Jumps Placed Side by Side

There will be many occasions on an agility course when your dog will be required to jump over one jump, turn 180 degrees, and take a second jump in the opposite direction.

Set up two jumps, side by side, with six to eight feet between them. The jump on your left is jump 1, and the jump on your right is jump 2.

Step 1

Start with your dog on your left about eight feet from jump 1. Tell him, "Go jump," signal with your left arm, and start running toward the jump. You will probably need to pass between the uprights of the two jumps. As your dog is in mid-air, start turning your body to the right and say, "Come." Keep your left hand extended from your side, to signal to him to remain on your left. Complete the turn so that you are facing

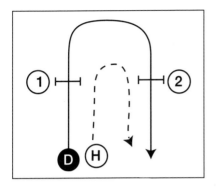

Figure 8-7. Introducing jump, turn, jump with dog on handler's left.

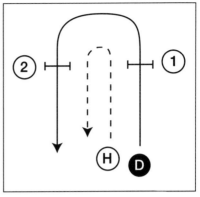

Figure 8-8. Introducing jump, turn, jump with dog on handler's right.

back the way you came. Tell him, "Go jump" and signal for him to take jump 2. Run back between the uprights toward your starting point. (See Figure 8-7.) Do not take your eyes off your dog. He may try to cut between the two jumps rather than jumping over the second jump. After a couple of repetitions, start over with him on your right. You will have him take jump 2, turn to the left, and then take jump 1. (See Figure 8-8.)

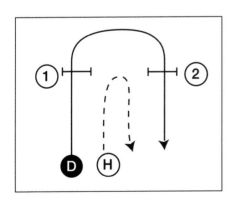

Figure 8-9. Handler remaining on the takeoff side of the jump.

Step 2

Repeat the previous exercise, but do not run as far forward between the uprights as you did previously. Try to have your dog take the two jumps while you stay on the takeoff side of jump 1. (See Figure 8-9.) This is a very basic jumping exercise, and eventually you will not find it necessary to go all the way between the uprights.

Two- and Three-Jump Variations

Step 3 (continued from previous section)

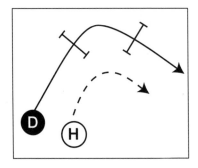

Figure 8-10. Jumps set in a V.

Place the two jumps in a V forma-
tion to make a 90-degree angle. The
inside uprights should be about eight
feet apart. Start with your dog on
your left. You should not have to pass
between the uprights in order for
your dog to take the second jump.
(See Figure 8-10.) Next, make the
jumps into
an inverted
V and move
the inside uprights to four feet apart. This is a
more difficult turn. Your dog will have to turn
270 degrees to take the second jump. You will
probably have to pass between the uprights as
you turn your dog toward the second jump.
(See Figure 8-11.) Gradually decrease the distance you have to travel between the uprights
until you can stay outside the uprights.

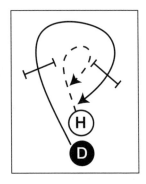

*Figure 8-11. Jumps set in
an inverted V. Dog makes
a 270-degree turn.*

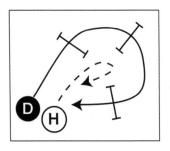

Figure 8-12. The pinwheel.

Step 4

Add a third jump. This is known as a
pinwheel, and this style of jump forma-
tion is found on almost every agility
course. Start with the jumps equidistant-
ly spaced, and then later vary the distance
and angles between the jumps. (See
Figure 8-12.)

Goal: To Have Your Dog Jump, Return to You, and Then Take a Second Jump in the Opposite Direction

Set up two jumps about eight feet apart, parallel to each other. Keep them low. The first jump you use will be jump 1; the second will be jump 2.

Step 1

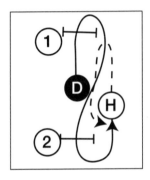

Figure 8-13. Jumping variations using two jumps.

With your dog off leash and on your left, stand between the jumps, facing jump 1. Signal toward jump 1 and say, "Go jump." Move with your dog toward the jump. As he is in mid-air, say, "Come," and as he lands, turn 180 degrees to your left and move toward jump 2. As your dog catches up to your right side say, "Go jump" and signal with your right arm toward jump 2. As he is in mid-air over jump 2, say, "Come" and step to the left to call him to you around the left jump upright. (See Figure 8-13.) Reward him. Repeat a couple of times and then start over with your dog on your right. He will turn to his left after taking jump 1, catch up to your left side then turn to his right after taking jump 2.

Step 2

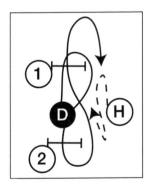

Figure 8-14.

Set up the previous exercise. With your dog on your left, send him over jump 1, turn 180 degrees to your left, call him, and send him over jump 2. As your dog is in mid-air over jump 2, call him and turn 180 degrees to your right. As he catches up to your left side, send him back over jump 1. Call him back to you around the right jump upright. (See Figure 8-14.)

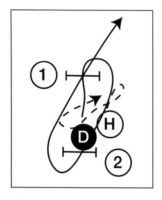

Figure 8-15.

Step 3

With your dog on your left, send him over jump 1 and then turn 180 degrees to your right to face jump 2. As your dog catches up to your left side, move laterally to your right and send him over jump 2. Again, turn to your right. Call him up to your left side, move laterally to the right and send him over jump 1 again. (See Figure 8-15.)

Step 4

Move the two jumps at right angles to each other. There should be about five feet between the inside uprights. The jump on the right is jump 1. Jump 2 is on the left, placed vertically to jump 1.

Face jump 1 and tell your dog to "Go jump," giving a signal with your left hand. As your dog is in mid-air, say, "Come." As he passes the right jump upright, turn to your left to face jump 2. Tell him, "Go jump" and signal with your right hand toward jump 2. When he is in mid-air over jump 2, step to the left and tell him, "Come." As he returns to you, turn to your right, to face jump 1. Send him back over jump 1. (See Figure 8-16.)

Repeat this exercise with jump 2 on your right. (See Figure 8-17.)

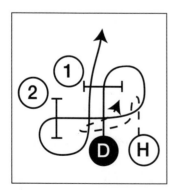

Figure 8-16.

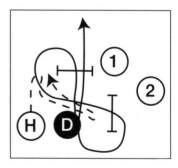

Figure 8-17.

Goal: To Teach a Turnback

There may be a time on an agility course when you need your dog to turn around and take some obstacle that is off to the side or behind him.

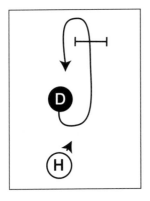

Figure 8-18. Turnback to the left.

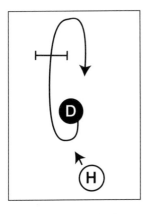

Figure 8-19. Turnback to the right.

Step 1

You should introduce this exercise by using only one jump in the beginning. Sit your dog facing you with his back to the jump. Place him about five feet in front of and to the left of a jump, as you stand facing it. Stand about four feet in front of him. Tell him, "Turn jump," and step toward the jump giving a signal with your right arm. Your dog should turn around to his left and run back to take the jump. As he is in mid-air over the jump, tell him to "come." Ideally, he should turn to the left and come around the left jump upright, back toward where you are standing. (See Figure 8-18.) After several successful repetitions, place him to the right of the jump and have him turn right to take the jump. (See Figure 8-19.) You will signal to the jump with your left arm. When your dog is turning in the correct direction every time after he takes the jump, move to step 2.

Step 2

Set up two jumps, side by side, with about eight feet between them. The jump on the left is jump 1, and the jump on the right, jump 2. The jumps are set up as they were when you first introduced your dog to a two-jump exercise. Position your dog, facing you, between the two

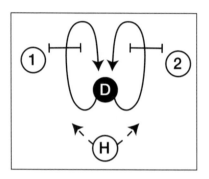

jumps, about five feet in front of the takeoff side. Tell him, "Turn jump" and signal to him to turn and take jump 1, by stepping toward it and signaling with your left arm. He should turn to his right and take the jump as he did in step 1. However, now he has a choice of which jump to take. Call him back to you between the jump uprights. Have him sit, and then have him turn left and take jump 2. Call him back to you between the jump uprights. (See Figure 8-20.)

Figure 8-20. Teaching the turnback using two jumps.

Step 3

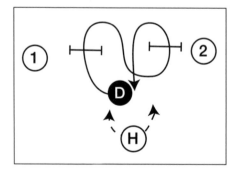

With the jumps set up as before, turn him to the right and send him over jump 1. Call him to you between the uprights, and while he is still moving, turn him to the left and send him over jump 2. Call him back between the uprights. (See Figure 8-21.)

Figure 8-21. Turnback, return through the middle of the jumps, then turnback again.

Step 4

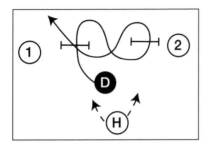

Figure 8-22. Turnback, return through the middle of the jumps, then turnback again, return through the middle again, and turnback once more.

Turn him to the right and send him over jump 1. Call him between the uprights and turn and send him over jump 2. Call him back through the uprights once more, and then turn him right and send him back over jump 1. (See Figure 8-22.)

Once your dog has mastered these jumping exercises, he will have learned a lot about your body language and should be able to turn tightly. You will probably also have learned a great deal about how easily you can send your dog over the wrong jump or why he fails to take a jump, based on the position of your body.

> **Any time your dog takes a wrong course, or has a refusal, immediately STOP and look at where your feet and body are pointing.**

You will soon discover that your body is giving your dog wrong information most of the time. This is one the hardest lessons for an obedience handler to learn. It is not so much what you tell your dog verbally that brings success on course, but what your body position is telling your dog. When you show in obedience, your dog responds to your verbal commands most of the time, and much of the time your body is stationary. In agility, both you and the dog are constantly moving, and he is watching for cues from your body.

Chapter 9

Taking a Running Start

In agility, your dog does not perform individual obstacles but sequences of obstacles.

Multiple Jump Sequencing

The easiest obstacles to begin sequencing are the jumps. Your dog already knows how to jump, whereas he may not know how to run through a tunnel or climb an A-frame and then stop in the contact zone. Therefore, you can introduce sequence training by using jumps while you are teaching your dog the correct way to perform the other obstacles. When he has been introduced to the spread and tire jumps, you can include them in your jumping sequence. Once he can correctly negotiate the tunnels, contacts, and weave poles, they too can be included in your sequencing. In the teaching phase, your dog should be jumping a lower height than he will be in competition.

Goal: To Call Your Dog over a Sequence of Four Jumps

Step 1

Place two jumps in line (parallel to each other) about fifteen to twenty feet apart, the distance between them being relative to the size of dog you are training. A small dog or a large, slow dog will need less space between the jumps than a fast dog. We will refer to the jump farthest from where you will be standing as jump 1 and the jump closest to you, jump 2. Place your dog sitting between the jumps, facing jump 2. Leave him on a "sit stay" and walk to the opposite side of jump 2. Notice that you are doing a "lead out"! Call him to you with the command, "Come jump." Reward him if he takes the jump. If he runs around the jump, say nothing, or say the word you use when you want to let him know he has made a mistake, and take him back to the start. If necessary, put on his leash. Do not move on to Step 2 until he is jumping well, off leash, over jump 2. If you have been practicing the exercises in Chapter 8, you should have no problem with your dog taking the jump.

Step 2

Sit him in front of jump 1. Position yourself immediately behind jump 2 on your dog's landing side. Call him by saying, "Come jump," and at the same time touch the top bar of jump 2. When he is in mid-air over jump 1, tell him again, "Come jump" and touch the top bar once more. Back up before your dog starts to take the second jump so that he has room to land. Reward him. Repeat this two-jump sequence several times.

Many dogs have no problem taking jump 1, but then run around jump 2. It is difficult to use a leash to correct this problem, as you might in obedience, because of the distance between you and your dog.

If you own baby gates that you use in obedience, you have the perfect solution.

Make a baby gate fence on both sides between the uprights of the jumps. Most obedience dogs are used to baby gates guiding them in obedience. They will not try to jump over them when they are used in this manner. If you do not have baby gates, go to a home improvement center and purchase some nylon mesh fencing and some stakes. Make a temporary fence on both sides of the jumps, similar to a jumping chute. When you think your dog has the idea of jumping two jumps, one after the other, move the jumps to a different location and see if he will jump the jumps without the fence for guidance. You may need to continue using the fence, so do not take it down until you are certain you no longer need it.

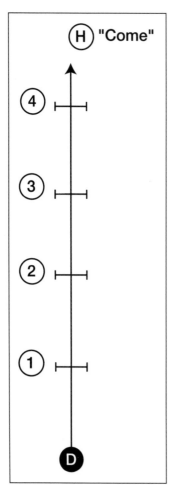

Step 3

Add a third jump if you have room. The jump farthest from you is jump 1, and the closest is jump 3. Sit your dog in front of jump 1, and go and stand on the landing side of jump 3. Call your dog, telling him, "Come jump." Repeat the command when he is in mid-air over jumps 1 and 2. If he jumps all three jumps, reward him. If you need to use baby gates or mesh fencing, do so.

Step 4

Add a fourth jump. Repeat the same procedure. Sit your dog in front of jump 1 and place yourself on the landing side of jump 4. (See Figure 9-1.)

When your dog can take all four jumps without any aids to keep him on track, the next step is to start running with him. Depending on your dog's ability, you might be able to do this by

Figure 9-1. Calling your dog over 4 jumps.

the end of your first training session, or it could take a number of training sessions to reach this stage. If you have been working the exercises using one and two jumps, in Chapter 8, your dog should have no problem with this.

There are no set rules for how quickly your dog learns in either obedience or agility.

When you start running with your dog, you will be sending him to a target. You should have already introduced your dog to targeting. If not, refer back to Chapter 6. The reason you are going to use a target is because you do not want your dog to jump with his head turned watching you as you run alongside him. You want him to look ahead toward the next obstacle. An obedience dog that has been taught attention work tends to watch his handler too closely. If you constantly reward your dog from your hand, you will encourage him to watch you rather than look where he is going. Think back to obedience. Many handlers spit food at their dogs on the recall to get them to look up at their face. With the use of a target, the dog becomes focused on what is ahead of him. At the beginning of sequence training, occasionally give him a treat from your hand, or pull a toy out of your pocket to toss to him. However, try to keep that to a minimum until he begins to look ahead for the next obstacle. Then you can dispense with the target and return to using a reward that comes from you. Agility is so self-rewarding that most dogs do not need as many rewards to motivate them as they do in obedience.

If you have room to set up four jumps, do so. This will allow you to continue working on the jumping sequence if you are making headway. If you only have room for two jumps, consider making a trip to the park! In the following sequence, if you have to train with only two jumps, jump 4 becomes jump 2, and jump 3 becomes jump 1.

Goal: To Run with and Send Your Dog over a Series of Four Jumps

Step 1

Sit your dog on the takeoff side of jump 4. Walk out and place the target about ten feet beyond the jump. Return to your dog, but stand off to the right of your dog so that you are positioned to the side of the jump upright/wing. When you begin the exercise, you will say to your dog, "Look. Go jump. OK, get it." This is exactly what you were doing when you taught targeting in Chapter 6, but you have now introduced a jump into the exercise and a jump command in addition to the command "go." The sequence will actually play out like this. Your dog is sitting facing jump 4. Say, "Look." When he is looking toward the target, say, "Go jump" and start running forward along the side of the right upright of jump 4, at the same time using your left arm to signal toward the jump. Your dog should start running toward the jump, and as he lifts off you should say, "OK, get it" as a cue for him to go to the target. Praise him. Repeat this a couple of times. If he does this successfully, then you are going to start over with him on your right. Do not forget, when your dog is on your right your signal will be given with your right arm.

> **Remember that you will always do more repetitions with your dog on your right than on your left.**

Step 2

Sit your dog on the takeoff side of jump 3. Remember, if you are only working with two jumps he will be sitting in front of jump 1. Place your target about ten feet beyond jump 4. Stand off to the right so that you are outside the uprights of jumps 3 and 4. Tell him, "Look" and then, "Go jump" as you start to run alongside the right upright of jump 3, at the same time giving him the signal to jump with your left arm. As he is in mid-air over jump 3, tell him again, "Go jump" and give another signal toward jump 4. As he lifts off over jump 4, tell him, "OK, get it" as a release to go to the target. After several repetitions, begin again with him on your right.

Step 3

If you are having no problem with him jumping two jumps with you running alongside him on both the right and the left, then add a third jump, and finally a fourth. (See Figure 9-2.) You may have found that by the time you reach this point you can no longer keep up with your dog. He is beating you down the line of jumps to get to the target at the end. This is exactly what you are looking for. You are now sending your dog over a sequence of jumps, a very important skill in agility.

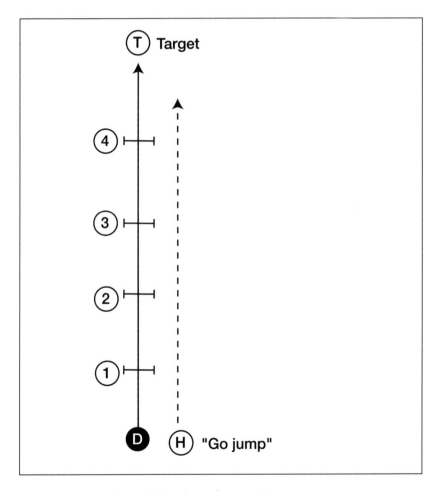

Figure 9-2. Send your dog over 4 jumps to a target.

Step 4

Make the jumping a little more complicated. Vary the distance between the four jumps and tilt them slightly so they are not parallel to each other. Then, stagger the jumps a little. Your dog must learn to move slightly to the right, or left, to take the next jump in line. You will rarely find jumps equally spaced and in a completely straight line on an agility course. (See Figure 9-3.)

Dealing with Refusals

What about the dog that wants to run next to you and misses the jump? This type of dog is known as a "Velcro" dog. Use your baby gates or nylon mesh fencing to place a barrier between the two of you. It should not take long for your dog to understand that he has to jump while you run alongside the jumps. As much as possible, stay well off the side of the jumps when you are running.

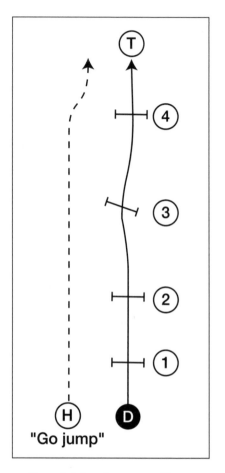

Figure 9-3. Jumping staggered jumps.

Agility jumps in trials often have wings, which force the handlers to stay away from the dogs. If you do not have baby gates or fencing or do not want to take the time to set them up, then run with your dog on leash if he is refusing jumps. A dog that is not trained with wings on the jumps is likely to miss the jump itself in competition because he is used to being closer to the handler. You would be wise to place an object alongside the jump uprights to force you to stay off to the side. Pushed-together baby gates work well for this. I have even seen them used in competition to make a wing jump.

When your dog is jumping a sequence of three or four jumps in a row, in a straight or staggered line, then it's time to throw him a curve.

Step 5 (continued from previous section)

Set the jumps in an arc. When the arc is to the right, you will run with your dog on your left. (See Figure 9-4.) He will have to travel farther than you will. Repeat with the jumps curving to the left. You will then have your dog on your right. Instead of moving the jumps reverse the direction you have been running. Reposition the target behind what once was jump 1 and start with your dog sitting in front of jump 4.

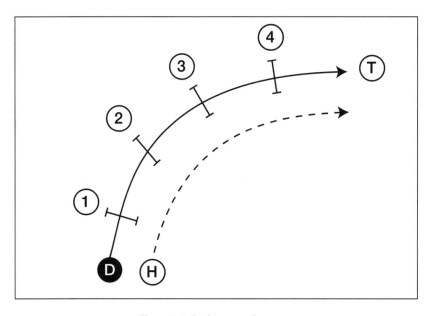

Figure 9-4. Set jumps up in an arc.

Remove the target once your dog is consistently taking a series of jumps in a straight line. Reward him occasionally with food from your hand or throw his toy. Return to using the target if you find your dog is watching you too closely and not looking ahead.

Call and Send

You have already introduced a similar exercise when you used two jumps in Chapter 8. A novice dog can benefit by learning the call and send. A typical scenario occurs when you send your dog into a tunnel. As he comes out, you may be ahead of him. You will need to call him to you and then send him on to another obstacle while you are both moving. Now is the time to refine this skill.

Goal: To Call Your Dog to You and Then Send Him on to Some More Obstacles

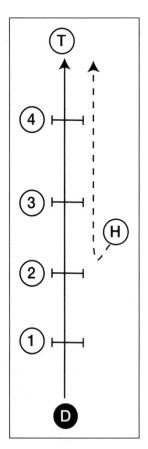

Figure 9-5. Call and send.

Step 1

Set up a line of four jumps, with your target placed beyond jump 4. Leave your dog sitting in front of jump 1, and go and stand off to the right midway between jumps 2 and 3, facing your dog. Call him over the first two jumps with the commands, "Come jump. Jump." As he is in the air over jump 2, pivot to your right 180 degrees to face jumps 3 and 4. Tell him, "Go jump. Go jump," and start to run, sending him over jumps 3 and 4 to his target. (See Figure 9-5.) Remember to turn in the direction you want your dog to go and never turn your back on your dog. By standing off to the right of the jumps, when you turn to your right and run with and send your dog on to jumps 3 and 4, he will be on your left, his comfort zone. Remove the target once he has grasped the concept of this exercise.

Step 2

Repeat while you stand to the left of the jumps. Turn 180 degrees to the left. This will position your dog on your right as you run toward jumps 3 and 4.

Change of Direction

Goal: To Teach Your Dog to Turn Right and Left on a Course

When your dog is reliably taking a sequence of jumps, it is time to teach him to jump, turn, and then jump again. You have already practiced this using only two jumps in Chapter 8.

Step 1

Position jumps 1 and 2 about fifteen to eighteen feet apart. Put jump 3 about ten feet beyond jump 2 and about eight feet off to the right, at a right angle to jumps 1 and 2. Place your target about ten feet beyond jump 3. With your dog on your left tell him, "Go jump," and start running alongside the uprights of jumps 1 and 2. As your dog is in the air over jump 2, say, "Come" and start turning toward jump 3. As your dog lands and starts to make the change in direction, signal to jump 3 with your left arm and say, "Go jump." Continue past the jump toward the target. As your dog is in mid-air over jump 3, say, "OK, get it." (See Figure 9-6.) Repeat this sequence a couple of times.

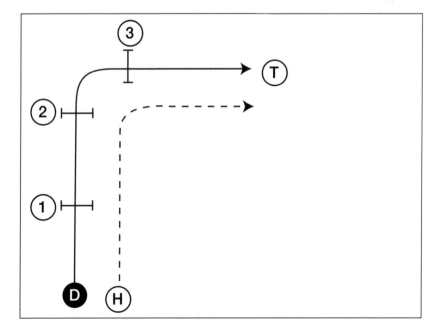

Figure 9-6. Introducing a change of direction.

Step 2

Move jump 3 to the left of jumps 1 and 2. Your dog will be on your right when you practice making left turns. You may run into a problem because, as you turn left, your dog may try to cut behind you and get into "heel" position. Be sure to pay attention to where your dog is heading after he lands following jump 2.

Step 3

When he is successfully making both turns, add a second jump after the turn so that he will be jumping two jumps, turning, and taking two more jumps. Remove the target and go to a schedule of random reinforcement.

If you are training a fast dog and you do not make the turn toward jump 3 soon enough, your dog may run past the left upright of jump 3, missing the jump entirely. If your dog moves slowly and you turn too soon, you will pull your dog to the right of jump 3. You have to experiment to see when you should start to make your turn. Your style of handling in agility depends a great deal on the type of dog you are training. Slow dogs often increase their speed when they gain confidence. Some dogs run differently in practice than they do in competition, when their adrenaline starts flowing.

With this last exercise, there was no jump in front of your dog when you made the turn. You now need to introduce a "call-off."

Goal: To Call Your Dog out of a Sequence of Jumps

Set up a line of four jumps, if possible. Put additional space between the jumps so your dog will have plenty of time to respond to your command to "come" without having the temptation of a jump immediately in front of him. If you have room, place the jumps about twenty feet apart.

Step 1

Place a target beyond the last jump. Run with your dog and send him over the four jumps to the target.

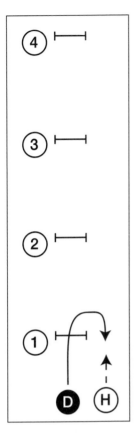

Figure 9-7. Call-off after one jump.

Step 2

Begin again at jump 1. This time, do not place a target out beyond jump 4. Tell your dog, "Go jump." When he is in mid-air over jump 1, tell him, "Come" and step sideways away from the line of jumps. (See Figure 9-7.) Make sure he does not back jump. If he turns and comes to you, reward him with a lot of praise and play. In Chapter 8 you practiced calling your dog back to you after he had taken only one jump. (See Figures 8-1 and 8-2, in Chapter 8.)

Step 3

Set out your target and start running with your dog down the line of jumps. Do not replace the target.

Step 4

Send your dog out over jumps 1 and 2, running with him but allowing him to move ahead of you. As he is in mid-air over jump 2, step away from the line of jumps and call him to you. Reward him.

Step 5

Replace the target and run with him down the line of jumps.

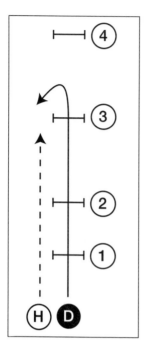

Figure 9-8. Call-off out of line of 4 jumps, at speed.

Step 6

Send your dog ahead of you over three jumps and then call him to you when he is in mid-air over jump 3.

Step 7

Repeat the previous exercises with your dog on your right. (See Figure 9-8.)

Why do you start calling him back to you early in the jump sequence in the beginning? You call him after only one jump so that his chance of responding will be greater because he is not moving as fast as he would be by the end of the sequence. As your dog begins to understand what you want, practice calling him when he is traveling at greater speed.

You do not place a target out when you are practicing the "call-off. " You do not want to reward your dog if he does not come when you call him. If there is a target out and he ignores your call, he will be rewarded for ignoring you. If your dog thinks he is supposed to always take the jump that is directly in his path and does not respond to your call, you will need to practice this with your dog on leash. Remember that if you put him on leash, he should be wearing a buckle collar.

Call-off, Turn, and Jump

You have taught the "call-off" and the "jump-turn-jump" as separate exercises. Now it is time to combine them. This is rather like adding the "stay" to the recall in obedience.

Goal: To Run with Your Dog, Call Him out of a Sequence of Jumps, and Send Him in a New Direction

Set up a line of three jumps. The distance between jump 1 and 2 should be about fifteen to eighteen feet. Place a third jump about twenty-five feet beyond jump 2. We will call this jump 3B. You can now see why you need to allow about sixty feet for training jumping exercises. Position jump 3A to the right of the line of jumps, as you did in the earlier exercise when you introduced the turn.

Step 1

Start with your dog on your left in front of jump 1. Tell him, "Go jump," signal, and start to run with him toward jump 1. When he is in mid-air over jump 1, tell him, "Go jump" and continue running forward toward jump 2. When he is in mid-air over jump 2, say, "Come" and start turning toward jump 3A. As soon as he is making a change of direction, signal toward jump 3 and tell him, "Go jump." (See Figure 9-9.) Why put jump 3B so far from jump 2 in the straight line of jumps?

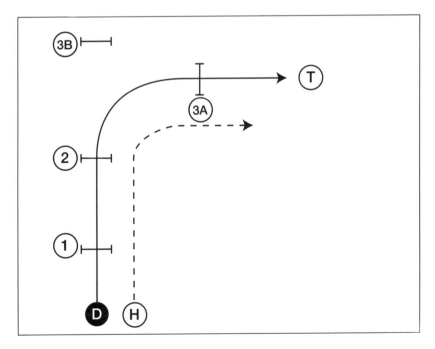

Figure 9-9. Call-off, turn, and jump.

Because you do not want your dog to be tempted by the off-course jump, 3B. Once he understands this new concept, then you can reduce the distance the off-course jump is placed from jump 2. Repeat the call-off, turn, and jump a couple of times.

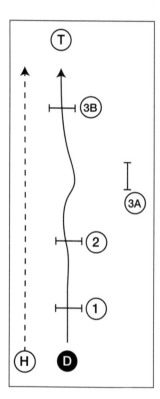

Figure 9-10. Working on anticipation.

Step 2

Position your target beyond jump 3B and send him straight down the line of jumps. (See Figure 9-10.) There is a very good chance that he will start to outguess you and begin to make the turn to jump 3A. Be sure to say, "Go jump" when he is in mid-air over jump 2. It might be better to have him run on your right down the line of jumps so that if he starts to anticipate turning right you can give him a "come" command to get him back on track. If he is on your left and starts turning to his right, you might collide with each other. Neither of you needs a bad experience at this point in your training.

Step 3

Repeat by placing jump 3A to the left of the line of jumps. Run with your dog on your right, turning left after jump 2. When it comes time for you to send your dog down the line of jumps to 3B, put out the target and switch to having him run on your left.

When you introduce the turn, if your dog wants to continue straight ahead over the off-course jump, do not hesitate to clap your hands to get his attention. You may even use his name to focus his attention on what you are doing. Although it is preferable to teach your dog to respond to your first command, you are not required to give only one command in agility, as you are in obedience. You need to condition yourself to give more than one command to your dog if it becomes necessary and even throw in a "stop" word if you need to do so. This element of the transition is the hardest for obedience exhibitors to accept. For years, obedience exhibitors have been conditioned to give their dogs one command only to do something.

Call, Turn, and Send

At the upper levels of agility, you are likely to be presented with the following handling challenge. The course will begin with a sequence of jumps, with a turn in front of an off-course obstacle. A good way to handle this challenge is for you to lead out and stand in front of the off-course obstacle. You will then be in a position to call your dog to you and, as he lands, turn and send him in the new direction. Your body will effectively block the off-course obstacle.

Goal: To Call Your Dog, Turn Him, and Send Him in a New Direction

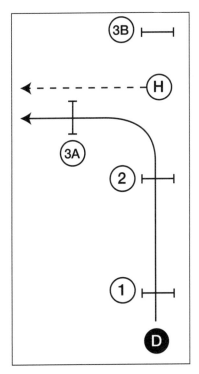

Set up the jumps as in the previous exercise, with jump 3A on the left.

Step 1

Leave your dog on a "stay." Lead out to a point between jumps 2 and 3B so that you are standing with your back to jump 3B, blocking your dog's view of that jump. Tell him to, "Come jump. Jump," and as he is in mid-air over jump 2, turn 90 degrees to your right and start moving toward jump 3A. Tell him, "Come," and then, "Go jump" and signal him to take jump 3A. (See Figure 9-11.) When you make the 90-degree turn to your right, it will put your dog on your left. Repeat this sequence several times.

Figure 9-11. Call, turn, and send.

Step 2

Move jump 3A to the right of the line of jumps. When you turn to send your dog in the new direction, you will be turning to your left. This will place your dog on your right.

Step 3

Add a jump after jump 3A so that you are calling your dog over two jumps and then sending him over two more jumps.

Be sure to place your dog on a schedule of random reinforcement. Your dog should be getting the idea of looking ahead, so you should no longer need to use a target. Sometimes reward him with a treat or toy that you carry on your body. Sometimes just praise and play with him. Keep treats or toys in your pocket, not in something obvious like a fanny pack or bait bag. You cannot wear one in the agility ring.

Now, stop using the word, "Look." From now on, you will only say, "Go jump," even if you are using a target. Only tell your dog to "Get it" if you are using a target or if you throw something for him to chase after.

The Speed Circle

The speed circle consists of several jumps set in a circle with unequal distances between the jumps and varying approach angles. With a speed circle, there is no beginning or end. You can have your dog jump one or two jumps in the circle, the entire circle, or several times around the circle. Initially you will run close to your dog until he understands this new exercise. As he gains more confidence, you will start moving toward the center of the circle. Eventually you will be turning in place while your dog is taking the jumps. Practice a "call-off" by calling him to you from various points within the circle (see Figure 9-12) and then reverse the direction he is jumping so that he is working off both your left and your right sides. Ultimately you can include the panel, tire, and spread jumps as part of the speed circle, not necessarily all at the same time.

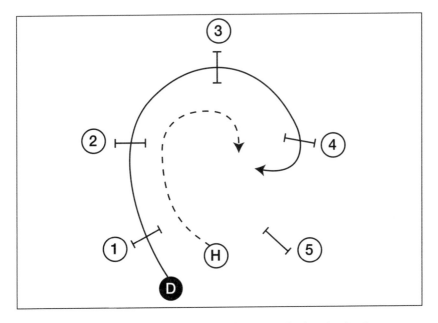

Figure 9-12. The speed circle. Calling the dog to you after he takes four jumps.

Panel Jump

This is almost exactly the same as an obedience high jump, except the boards can be easily dislodged. You can include the panel jump (or your obedience high jump) in your jumping sequence at any time.

Raising Jump Heights

As your dog gets more experienced in taking sequences of jumps, it is advisable to slowly raise the jumps to full height. You certainly do not need to practice all the time at full height, and you may not wish to do so if you are training an older dog. When a dog is jumping lower than required, his timing and turning is likely to be different. You need to run him periodically at the height he is going to jump in competition so that you can get a feel for how you will need to handle him in the ring. Some dogs are lazy and need to be reminded to pick up their feet. If you let them jump lower than required in training, they will tend to take bars down in competition. If you are practicing with your dog jumping full height, do it at the start of the training session when your dog is fresh and then lower the jumps for additional training.

Chapter 10

The Broad Jump (and Spread Jumps) Revisited

The Broad Jump

Obstacle commands for the broad jump are usually the same as those for your regular jump, with the word big sometimes added.

If you trained your dog in open obedience, he will already have been introduced to the broad jump. In agility, you see two different styles of broad jump. The one you are used to seeing is the obedience-style broad jump, with the board heights placed in ascending order. This style of broad jump can only be taken in one direction. The other style of broad jump is a hogback variety, where the height of the boards ascends and descends from front to back. If you ever decide to buy a broad jump strictly for agility, get the hogback variety because it can be jumped from both directions. This is useful because, if you need to reverse direction in a jumping sequence, you will not have to turn the broad jump around. The biggest difference between the broad jump in obedience and the broad jump in agility is that the agility jump has a pole in each corner. The poles make the jump more visible to the dog, and it is easier for the judge to see if the dog has cleared the entire span.

Before anyone ever thought of agility competition, I trained my obedience dogs to jump the broad jump by placing a cone on both sides of the first board. It is easy for a dog to miss seeing the broad jump because it lies so flat. A high jump has uprights on which the dog can focus, so I made it easy for my dogs to focus on the broad jump through the use of cones.

I never wanted my dogs to consider tiptoeing through the broad jump. From day one, I used chicken wire tents (1′ × 4′ or 2′ × 4′ sections of chicken wire folded in half, lengthwise) placed in the spaces between the boards. If you train a small dog, you will only need one piece. It is miserable stuff to move around, so small dog trainers are lucky. I have never placed a bar jump in between the broad jump boards. I feel it changes the picture of the broad jump too much. A dog needs to learn what a broad jump looks like right from the beginning. Chicken wire does not radically change the appearance of a jump. The chicken wire will make the dog arc higher over the jump, and you would be wise to use it in practice. Some dogs spook when they first see chicken wire between the boards. Introduce it one piece at a time.

Goal: To Introduce the Broad Jump into the Jumping Sequence

Step 1

Leave your dog and call him over the broad jump. Your dog may not be used to you standing on the opposite side of the broad jump.

Step 2

Place your target out about ten feet beyond the last broad jump board. With your dog on your left, stand to the right of the jump. Tell your dog, "Look," "Go jump," and "OK, get it" as he is in mid-air over the jump. By now, he should be used to the targeting game, and you should be able to progress quite quickly.

Step 3

Add the broad jump to your jump sequencing, starting out with it being the first jump in line. Then move the broad jump between and after your single bar jumps. Do not place the broad jump as the first jump after a turn because it is easy for a dog to cut a corner of the jump. You need to make him square up when he takes any spread jumps. If your dog jumps any spread jump at an angle, he will have to jump a greater distance, possibly hitting a board or displacing a bar. If you are practicing the sequence of *two jumps, turn, two jumps,* the broad jump can be placed as the second jump after the turn. By the time your dog has taken the first jump after the turn, he should be lined up for a straighter approach to the broad jump.

When you include the tire and panel jumps in your sequencing, place the broad jump both before and after those jumps. The more experience your dog has in jumping the broad jump in a sequence of different types of jumps, the more likely he will be to notice it at a trial.

The Double Bar Jump

If you made your single bar jumps according to the directions in Appendix B, one of your single bar jumps will be narrower than the other jumps. If you have a dog that jumps sixteen inches or more, you can use that particular jump as the first section of the double bar jump by placing it in front of another single bar jump. If you use jumps of identical width, the feet of the jumps will not allow you to set the spread correctly because they will interfere with each other. If you have a smaller breed, then you will need to make two uprights using five-way crosses so that you can make the spread less than eight inches. With a double bar jump, the jump bars are set parallel to each other, and the width of the spread is half the height of the jump. A double bar jump really should not cause your dog any problems. However, if you should happen to cross behind your dog when he is taking that jump, he may look back at you. This could cause him to drop a leg and take down one of the bars. When you introduce the double bar jump, use it first as an individual jump. Later place the double bar jump as one of the jumps in straight-line sequencing. Finally, position this jump before and after turns and use it in the speed circle.

The Triple Bar Jump

This jump causes the most grief on an agility course. For some reason, the triple bar is often the last jump of the advanced level course and has to be taken when your dog might be getting tired. It has been my nemesis on many an occasion when running my older dog. You will not find the triple in novice competition. It is not an easy jump to build yourself. However, you will find a triple bar jump fits nicely into a Christmas stocking!

By the time you introduce your dog to the triple, he should be comfortable jumping with you running beside him on either side and be successful at clearing the double bar jump. Start with the jump low and always approach the jump straight on, as you do the broad jump. When you are running a course, try not to cross behind at the triple. You want your dog to concentrate on the jump and not start looking to see where you might be heading.

There is some disagreement in agility circles about how to handle the approach to the triple. Some trainers recommend pushing your dog toward the jump so he takes it at speed, because it is a spread jump as well as a high jump and he needs velocity to get over it. I have found that it is often better to slow my dog down and have him take the jump under more control. You have to know how your dog jumps. Pushing a dog for speed can flatten your dog's trajectory over a jump, which is the last thing you want to do with the triple. Dogs that jump flat tend to take down bars, and the triple has three of them just waiting for your dog to make a mistake.

After you have introduced your dog to the triple jump, place it as one of the jumps in your straight-line jumping sequence or when your dog is jumping in a curved line. Next, use it before a turn. Finally, add it after a turn. Be sure to leave extra space between the triple and the jump preceding it so that your dog has a chance to square up on the approach to the triple jump.

Chapter 11

Jumping Through Hoops

Obstacle commands for the tire jump are usually "tire," "hoop," "circle," or "through."

For the novice agility dog, particularly a dog with an obedience background, the tire jump is probably the most difficult jump to perfect in the early stages of training. You see more refusals on the tire jump in novice agility than on any other type of jump. With ring experience, most dogs appear to overcome the problem. Obedience dogs have learned to clear jumps, and some want to jump over the whole tire jump, frame and all. Others do not seem to understand jumping through the center of the tire and try to jump between the frame and the tire itself. Certain breeds showing in obedience always jump alongside the uprights rather than the center of the high and bar jumps. These dogs may have a hard time learning the tire.

The tire jump is one piece of equipment you would be wise to own. It is also a good idea to get your dog used to jumping through different tires and frames. Perhaps you can trade tires with a training partner. Tires come in different colors and striping. Often an inexperienced dog does not recognize the tire on the course for what it is, if it looks different from what he is used to seeing in training. Remember that dogs are context-oriented. This probably accounts for the reason why so many novice dogs incur a refusal on the tire jump in the ring. You should teach your dog to jump through a twenty-inch tire in practice. A dog is less likely to fail to jump through a twenty-four-inch tire if he is used to jumping through a twenty-inch tire, rather than the other way around. The smaller the tire, the more likely your dog is to brush against the sides when jumping. He should get used to brushing against the tire so that if he hits one in competition he will not get spooked.

Goal: To Teach Your Dog to Jump Through the Center of the Tire

I like to start teaching the dog to jump the tire when he is on leash. Set the height of the tire quite low, no matter how high your dog is jumping the single bar jumps. You are only interested in conditioning the dog to come to you through the center of the tire. You do not care if he jumps through it or simply steps through it, so you can initially have the bottom of the tire resting on the ground if you train a small dog.

Step 1

Leave your dog on a "sit stay" on one side of the tire jump and walk to the other side. Pass your leash through the center of the tire so the leash is running directly from your dog's collar to your hand. I have found that a dog will actually follow the direction in which the leash is going. Pat the inside bottom part of the tire to focus your dog's attention on this new piece of equipment. Tell him, "Come, jump" (or "tire"). Back up so you do not block his path through the tire. I usually tell my dog to "jump" in the beginning. I find the word association with jumping is helpful until the dog becomes familiar with jumping through the middle of the tire. Once he understands the exercise, then give the tire a name. Be sure that in the beginning you always have the dog lined up and centered on the tire. If your dog approaches the tire at an angle, the center will appear visibly smaller, and he is much more likely to hit the sides, possibly giving him a bad experience. (See Figures 11-1 and 11-2.)

Figure 11-1. The center of the tire appears wide with a straight-on approach. Cones fill space between bottom and sides of tire.

Figure 11-2. Center of tire appears narrower with an angled approach.

Step 2

When your dog is reliably jumping through the middle of the tire, raise the height a couple of inches. Most tires can be raised an inch at a time. If you raise the tire slowly, your dog is less likely to notice the change, and you should have fewer problems with him wanting to run underneath it. Your biggest challenge will be preventing him from trying to jump between the sides of the tire and the tire frame. When you have him actually jumping through the center, you can remove the leash, but be ready to replace it if you have problems. Once he is off leash, you can increase the distance you sit him in front of the tire.

Step 3

Place your target about ten feet beyond the tire. With your dog on your left, send him to jump through the tire while you run alongside him like you did when you started sequencing with the single bar jumps. Do not forget to give your hand signal. You cannot run with your dog on leash since the leash will get tangled around the tire frame. After several repetitions, start running with your dog on your right.

Raise the tire some more, slowly, slowly! A dog needs to figure out exactly how to get through the center of the tire without banging into it. Most trainers recommend that once a dog is jumping his full height on the tire, it should remain at that height. Do not lower the tire, as you might lower the other jumps to prevent a dog from getting tired when doing multiple jumps.

Goal: To Introduce the Tire into a Jumping Sequence

When your dog is confidently jumping through the tire on both a recall and a run-by, it is time to add the tire jump to your sequence of jumps.

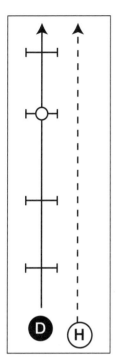

Figure 11-3. Adding a tire to a line of jumps.

Step 1

Start out with a straight line of jumps. Have your dog jump the tire and then two or three single bar jumps. Switch the tire and the succeeding bar jumps. (See Figure 11-3.) Now he will be jumping a bar jump before and after the tire. Finally, have him jump two or three bar jumps and then the tire.

Step 2

Start working on your turns with the tire jump placed both before the turn and, later, after the turn. (See Figures 11-4 and 11-5.)

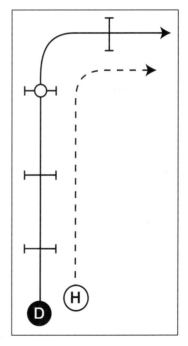

Figure 11-4. Place a tire before a turn.

What can you do to prevent your dog from either running under the tire as the height is raised or attempting to jump between the tire and the frame? If your dog tries to run under the tire, place a piece of chicken wire below the tire (a 1′ × 4′ or 2′ × 4′ section folded in half lengthwise works well). He will run into the wire if he tries to cheat. You do not want him to hurt himself should he try to go under and not through the center of the tire. Nylon mesh fencing also works well. You would need to tie the fencing to the frame and the bottom of the tire. To

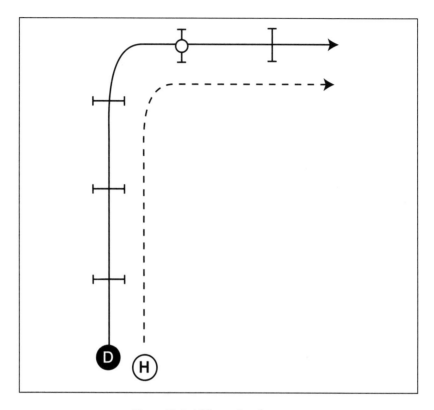

Figure 11-5. Adding a tire after a turn.

prevent a dog from jumping between the tire and the frame, place a traf-fic cone on both sides of the tire to fill the space between the tire and the frame. You can also place smaller cones between the bottom of the tire and the frame, to prevent your dog from running underneath, in place of chicken wire. (See Figure 11-1.) When your dog is fully confident jumping through the tire and is only making a few mistakes, you can use plastic kitchen wrap underneath the tire or between the tire and the frame. The plastic wrap should be fairly invisible to your dog and should really take him by surprise if he tries to run under the tire or jump between the tire and the frame. You should not use this technique until you are convinced your dog knows what he is supposed to do but is choosing not to do it. If you have a dog that is easily spooked, this is probably not the right solution for you. A bad experience with an obstacle may make your dog try to avoid it altogether. In this case, you would be better off using something more visible, like mesh fencing or small cones, to deter your dog from jumping anywhere but through the center of the tire.

> **Remember that the tire itself can frame a succeeding obstacle. Sometimes it is the one you wish the dog to take, but the tire can also frame an off-course obstacle.**

Chapter 12

Moving Beyond Basics

When your dog has more experience jumping, there are some advanced handling techniques that you need to practice in order to run a course successfully. It is unlikely you will need them in novice standard, but you will certainly need them in the advanced standard and the jumpers classes.

Goal: To Teach the Dog to Move Sideways, Away from You, to Take a Jump

There will be places on an agility course where the next obstacle is not immediately in front of your dog, but off to one side. In addition, the obstacle in your dog's path may not be the next one in the sequence. The command you will be using is "Get out." It was introduced in Chapter 5.

Step 1

Place two single bar jumps parallel to each other, about twenty feet apart. Jump 2 will be offset to the left about four feet to the side of jump 1. Start with your dog on your left. Tell him, "Go jump" and signal toward jump 1 with your left arm. As your dog is in mid-air over jump 1, say, "Get out, jump." You need to turn your dog away from you, so give the signal for jump 2 with your right arm. This is one occasion when you do not signal with the arm that is closest to the obstacle. When you signal in this way, your entire body will turn. This makes it easier for your dog to understand the change in direction. As you tell him to "get out," you can move slightly in the direction of jump 2. Since there is no other jump he can take, he should have no trouble understanding what you want. After he has taken jump 2, call him to you, and reward him. (See Figure 12-1.) Repeat several times, and then move jump 2 to the right of jump 1. Run with your dog on your right. Give the signal to "get out" with your left arm. Shorten the distance between the jumps so that the angle your dog has to take to get over jump 2 is a little sharper, and start over with your dog on your left (Figure 12-2).

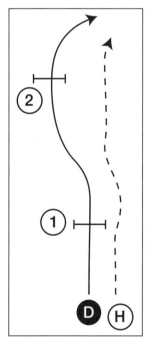

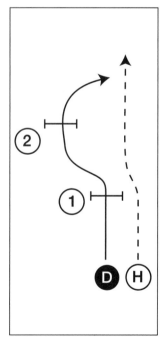

Figure 12-1. Teaching the "get out."

Figure 12-2. Sharpen the angle.

Step 2

Add a third jump. Jumps 1 and 3 will be in line with each other. Jump 2 will be offset to the left. Run with your dog on your left, send him over jump 1, and then have him "Get out" over jump 2. As he is in mid-air over jump 2, call him toward you. Then send him over jump 3, giving the signal for jump 3 with your left arm. (See Figure 12-3.) He has to learn to listen to what you say and not go on autopilot. Therefore, when you start the sequence again, you will not send him over jump 2. Instead, you will bypass jump 2 and send him over jump 1 and then jump 3. (See Figure 12-4.) Mix it up. Sometimes have him "get out" to a jump out of line, and at other times have him ignore that jump and run in a straight line instead. Do not forget to work him from both sides.

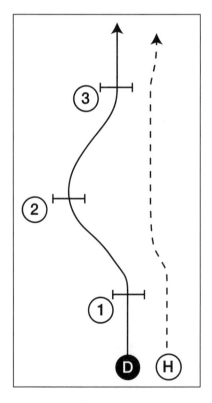

Figure 12-3.

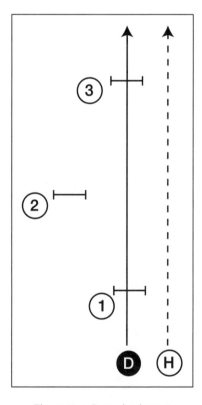

Figure 12-4. Bypassing jump 2.

Step 3

If you have the space, set out five jumps. Jumps 1, 3, and 5 will be in line, and jumps 2 and 4 will be offset on the same side. When you practice with five jumps, you can have him jump all five, skip jump 2, or skip jump 4, or just jump 1, 3, and 5. This will really teach your dog to listen to what you tell him.

Eventually, once your dog has mastered the tunnel and the table, you can incorporate them in this sequence. He will need to learn to "get out" to other obstacles in addition to a jump.

Goal: To Switch Sides While Running with Your Dog

In agility, it is almost impossible to have your dog run on the same side throughout the entire course. In the advanced classes, there will be many occasions when you will need to switch sides while both you and your dog are moving. This maneuver is called a "dynamic cross." You can cross in front of your dog's path or behind your dog's path. The safest way to switch sides is by crossing in front of your dog. When you cross in front of your dog, he can see what you are up to. However, a "cross in front" is only possible when you are ahead of your dog. If you have been teaching the tunnel, contacts, and table, you will have already introduced your dog to a change in sides, albeit a static or blind side switch.

Goal: To Introduce the "Cross in Front"

Step 1

Set up two rows of two jumps. The rows should be spaced about six feet apart, and the two jumps in each row, about eighteen feet apart. The two jumps in the row on your left will be jumps 1 and 2. The jumps in the row on your right will be jumps 4 and 3, from front to back. You will begin this exercise standing between the two rows of jumps, with your dog on your left. Run with him, and send him to take jumps 1 and 2. As he is in mid-air over jump 2, call and turn him and have him take jumps 3 and 4. (See Figure 12-5.) You have previously practiced something similar using only two jumps, in Chapter 8. (See Figures 8-7, 8-8, and 8-9.) Repeat this exercise with your dog on your right. He will start by taking jumps 4 and 3, then turn and take jumps 2 and 1.

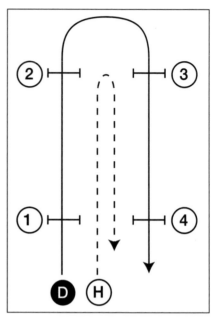

Figure 12-5. Setting up for the "cross in front."

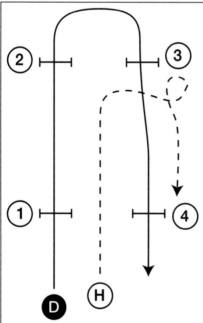

Figure 12-6. The "cross in front."

Step 2

To introduce the "cross in front," you will begin again with your dog on your left. Run with him and send him over jumps 1 and 2. However, you will hang back and not run with him up to jump 2. Instead, as he approaches jump 2, you will move laterally to your right to stand facing the landing side of jump 3. As your dog lands after jump 2, call him to you over jump 3. As he is in mid-air over jump 3, turn to your left to face jump 4 and start moving forward. Signal toward jump 4 with your right arm and say, "Go jump." Your dog will now be running on your right. (See Figure 12-6.) Repeat this exercise several

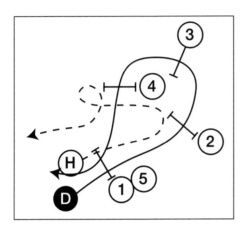

times, and then switch to running with your dog on your right. Send him over jumps 4 and 3. Move laterally to your left to face the landing side of jump 2. Call your dog over jump 2, and when he is in mid-air turn to your right to face jump 1. Send your dog toward jump 1. Your dog will now be on your left.

You will often use a "cross in front" when there is a pinwheel on the course. (See Figure 12-7.)

Figure 12-7. "Cross in front" at the pinwheel.

Goal: To Introduce the "Cross Behind"

The "cross behind" can only be used if your dog is ahead of you. If you and he are running side by side and you try to cross behind him, one of two things is likely to happen. You and your dog may have a collision, (Chapter 5, Figure 5-4) or he will move laterally away from you to avoid running into you. Should this happen, he is likely to go off course, or incur a refusal. Perfect timing of a "cross behind" is essential for it to work correctly.

Step 1

Set up a line of three jumps. The distance between jumps 1 and 2 should be about fifteen to eighteen feet. Place a third jump about twenty-five feet beyond jump 2. We will call this jump 3B. Position jump 3A at a right angle to the line of jumps, about fifteen feet beyond jump 2 and about eight feet off to the side. With your dog on your right, run with him and send him down the line of three jumps. You practiced this exercise in Chapter 9 when you practiced a "call-off."

Step 2

With your dog on your right, run with him and send him over jumps 1 and 2. Start to hang back as your dog approaches jump 2 so that he is moving well ahead of you. As he lifts off over jump 2 say, "Switch, come" and cross to the right side of jump 2. Continue moving toward jump 3A. (See Figure 12-8.) It is probable that your dog will spin on landing after jump 2. (See Figure 12-9.) He does not expect you to be on his right. Repeat this sequence several times until your dog lands after jump 2 and smoothly turns right. Have him take jump 3A and reward him. Next, run down the line of jumps to jump 3B with your dog still on your right. (Refer to Figure 9-10.) You want him to pay attention to what you are doing and not decide to make a turn on his own.

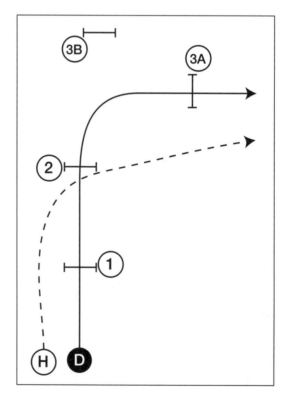

Figure 12-8. The "cross behind" with the dog turning correctly.

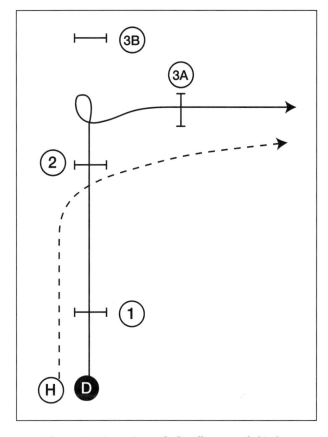

Figure 12-9. Dog spins as the handler crosses behind.

Step 3

Move jump 3A to the left of the line of jumps. Repeat the same procedure with your dog running on your left. You will cross behind him,
to your left, before you reach jump 2.

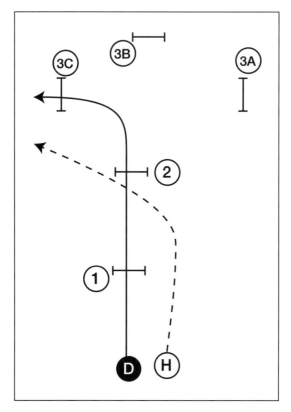

Figure 12-10. Handler runs with dog on left and then crosses behind and turns the dog left.

Step 4

Place a jump both to the left and right of jump 2. (See Figures 12-10 and 12-11.) Call these jumps 3A and 3C. Now you can run with your dog and do a simple turn to the left, or right, or practice a "cross behind." He will never know what is expected. Vary the exercise by having him turn after jump 2 or send him straight down the line of jumps over 3B.

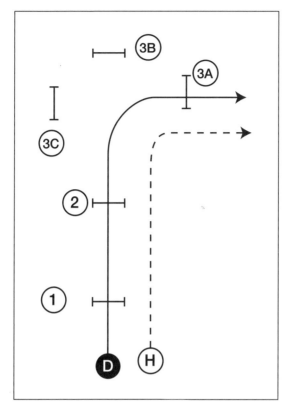

Figure 12-11. Handler runs with dog on left and then turns right to work on anticipation.

Goal: To Introduce the Jumping Square

The jumping square is usually found in jumpers courses. You should introduce this concept before you start entering your dog in trials. Four jumps are set up to make a square. When a jumping square is used on a course, your dog will most likely cross through it several times. Dogs remember where they have previously been and often try to go the same way again. You have probably run into that very thing in utility. If your dog goes out to the corner on one "go out," he will very likely go there on the second one. With the jumps in the square so close together, your dog can go off course before you realize it.

You have already introduced your dog to many of the possible combinations used in the jumping square when you practiced with only two jumps in Chapter 8.

Set your jumps in a square with about eighteen feet between them. The two jumps straight ahead are jumps 1 and 2. The jump to the right is jump 3, and the one opposite jump 3 is jump 4.

Step 1

With your dog on your left, run with him and send him over jumps 1 and 2. Turn 270 degrees to the right and have him take jump 3. Then cross the square and have him take jump 4. (See Figure 12-12.) Praise/reward. Repeat with your dog on your right. Turn him left after jump 2, and then send him over jump 4 to jump 3. Your dog will remain on the same side of you throughout this exercise.

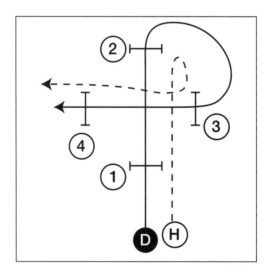

Figure 12-12. The jumping square.

Step 2

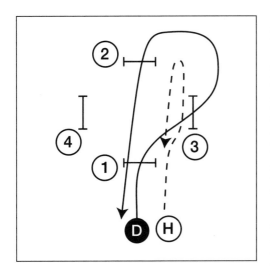

Figure 12-13.

With your dog on your left, have him take jump 1. Then turn him to take jump 3. As he lifts off to take jump 3, cross behind him in front of jump 3, turn him to the left, and have him take jump 2 back into the square. Send him out of the square over jump 1. (See Figure 12-13.) Repeat with him on your right. After he takes jump 1, turn him left to take jump 4 out of the square. Then cross behind him in front of jump 4. Next, turn him right and have him take jump 2 back into the square, and leave the square by taking jump 1.

Step 3

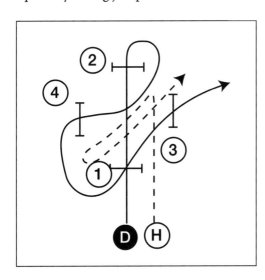

Figure 12-14.

With your dog on your left, send him over jumps 1 and 2. Call him back into the square around the right upright of jump 2. Next, turn and send him out of the square over jump 4, from your right. Turn him to the left and have him reenter the square by taking jump 1. Send him out of the square over jump 3 from your right. (See Figure 12-14.)

You can use the jumping square to practice all sorts of different sequences and turns. These are just a few examples of exercises to practice with a jumping square.

Jumping Jeopardy

Bars get displaced for many reasons. If a dog frequently takes down a bar on the final obstacle of the course, it is often the fault of the handler. This often happens at the end of a clean run, a major disappointment. Handlers prematurely celebrate their clean run just as their dog is in mid-air over the final jump. Their dog hears a commotion behind him and turns around to see what is happening. This causes him to drop a hind leg, and—bingo—the clean run is no more. Downed bars often happen when the handler crosses behind on a spread jump. The dog turns around to see where his handler went and drops a leg and a bar.

If a dog is not clearing the distance on the broad jump, or the double or triple, perhaps the dog is not approaching the jump straight on. Remember that a dog that jumps a spread jump at an angle will have to clear a greater distance than he would if he jumped it straight on. You may need to change his approach path.

PVC bars are light in weight, and some dogs pay no attention when they hit them. If you have an insensitive dog you might consider placing ¾-inch rebar inside the PVC jump bars. When your dog hits this bar, he is more likely to notice he made a mistake.

In some agility organizations, refusals are penalized. In others, they are not. Regardless of whether they are penalized or not, refusals cost time. Inexperienced handlers often pull their dogs off an obstacle by running directly at it, instead of running slightly to the side of it. As the handler steps to the side to get around the obstacle, or the wing of a jump, the dog follows the handler and incurs a refusal. In other cases, the handler may inadvertently step into his dog's path and push his dog away from the obstacle. This often occurs when the handler is planning on a "cross behind" and the dog is not far enough in front of the handler. The dog sees the handler moving toward him and moves out of the way, off to the side of the jump.

Refusals at the tire jump are more likely to be caused by the dog not recognizing the type of tire jump being used. Remember that dogs are context-oriented. The more exposure to different tires your dog gets, the less likely he will be to refuse to jump through one.

Hitting the boards of the broad jump is often caused because the dog never sees the jump. The "hogback-style" broad jump is easier to see than the obedience broad jump. You need to use the broad jump when practicing jumping exercises so your dog is aware that such an obstacle exists on the course.

Chapter 13

The Light at the End of the Tunnel

Tunnel commands are usually "tunnel," "through," "get in," "chute," and "rip."

For some reason, dogs appear to really enjoy going into tunnels. This might have something to do with the fact that dogs are den animals that seek out dark, confined places in which to live. Next to the pause table, tunnels are the easiest of all the agility obstacles to teach. The open or pipe tunnel is slightly easier to teach than the closed. The closed tunnel is often called the "collapsed" or "chute" tunnel. It comprises a barrel with an attached chute. Once your dog is familiar with running through the open tunnel, he should be less intimidated by the closed variety. Open tunnels come in varying lengths. You will usually see fifteen- and twenty-foot tunnels on an agility course.

Regular agility tunnels are heavy items that often take two people to move. You can buy children's play tunnels, but they are not large enough for many of the bigger breeds to run through. In addition, they are not very substantial, so they may not hold up well. If you decide to purchase a real agility tunnel, you might as well buy a twenty-foot one because you can use it in many more configurations than a fifteen-foot tunnel. The difference in cost is not that much; however, the larger the tunnel, the heavier it is to move!

If you are training an older dog, one thing to consider when sending your dog into a tunnel is that his eyes may not adjust to changes in light as quickly as the eyes of a younger dog. As your older dog comes out of a dark tunnel into the light, he may have to hesitate to regain his vision. This is particularly true of the collapsed tunnel where your dog is in total darkness until he emerges from the chute. Depending on the configuration of the open tunnel, he may be able to see daylight while running through it and therefore may be less blind as he exits.

The Open Tunnel

You will discover that when you train in agility you really need a training partner, much more than you do in obedience. You will need help moving the tunnel for a start! To begin, squash the tunnel together as much as possible so that your dog has only a short distance to go to reach the end. The tunnel should be straight and not curved. If you do not have a pipe tunnel, you may use the barrel of the chute tunnel to introduce this exercise. A pipe tunnel needs to be anchored to the ground so it cannot roll around as your dog runs through it. This can be accomplished quite easily by filling large plastic jugs with water or sand. Hook a bungee cord to the handle of each jug and place it over and around each end of the tunnel. Laundry detergent bottles work well for this.

You will need to work your dog on leash in the beginning, but do not use the type of leash you use in obedience. You will need something about six feet long but without a handle. A handle might hang up on some of the agility equipment. Go to the hardware store and purchase about six feet of fairly heavy nylon twist cord and a bolt snap. Burn both ends of the cord so they do not fray and attach the snap to one end.

Goal: To Call and Send Your Dog Through an Open Tunnel

Step 1

If you have a training partner, have her hold your dog on leash, immediately in front of one end of the tunnel, while you move to the opposite end. Be sure your dog is wearing a buckle collar. Squat down and talk to your dog, show him his motivator, and then call him to you. Your partner should only release your dog when his head is inside the tunnel. I suggest giving your dog his "kennel" command when you introduce the tunnel. It works well. Switch over to a tunnel command once he shows you that he really understands what you want. After a few repetitions, your partner should be able to allow your dog a little more leash. He should dive into the tunnel when you call him. Depending on the size of your dog, he may need to duck to get into the tunnel since he may stand taller than the tunnel entrance.

Step 2

Once your dog will come to you through the squashed-up tunnel, gradually extend the tunnel until it has attained its full length.

Step 3

Once your dog is running through the straight tunnel, add a slight bend. When the tunnel is straight, your dog can see out the other end. As the tunnel begins to curve, his view will be restricted. Your dog has to have confidence that there is an exit to the tunnel even if he cannot see it. He needs to be convinced that he is not going to run into something in the darkness. Eventually put a 90-degree bend in the tunnel.

Step 4

When your dog will run through the tunnel on command to reach you, start sending him through it to get his motivator.

How do you train the tunnel if you do not have a partner? Essentially, you send your dog through the tunnel to get his motivator. Either place the motivator at the exit end or throw it through the tunnel from the entrance end. If you throw the motivator, be sure it lands beyond the tunnel exit. You do not want your dog to stop once he is inside the tunnel. Do not let go of your dog's leash until he is committed to running through the tunnel to reach the motivator. You can also set up two baby gates, one on each side of the tunnel entrance, funneling your dog into the tunnel. Place him on a "sit stay," go to the other end, and call him. Because the baby gates prevent him from running past the tunnel entrance, he is likely to come through the tunnel to reach you.

A few dogs appear to be frightened of the tunnel, and sometimes the owners have to crawl into the tunnel before they can convince their dogs to come to them. *Never* force a dog into a tunnel if he is reluctant to go into it. If you have a dog like that, you may need to obtain a large cardboard box. Open both ends, and tape them back on themselves. Try to obtain a box about eighteen to twenty-four inches square. You may need to leave it on the kitchen floor for several days. Put your dog's feed bowl inside the box so he has to enter it to eat. Then untape one end to make it a little longer. Then untape the other end. Your dog should get over his fear if you take things slowly. Then feed him in the tunnel.

Goal: To Teach Your Dog to Find the Tunnel Entrance

Step 1

Place your motivator slightly beyond the tunnel exit. Hold your dog on leash, about three feet from the entrance, facing a full-length, straight tunnel. Give your dog his tunnel command. If he runs through without guidance, then hold him slightly to the right of the tunnel so that he has to enter by moving forward and to the left. Do not forget to release the leash as he commits to the tunnel entrance. Gradually increase the angle he has to take to enter the tunnel. Then send him into the tunnel from the left. He will be on your right. Stand farther back from the tunnel so that he has to go farther to reach the entrance. Remember that the opening of the tunnel will be less obvious when the dog is approaching it at an angle. It is the same as the tire jump, which looks smaller when the dog does not have a straight-on approach. (See Figures 13-1 and 13-2.)

Step 2

Send him to a curved tunnel but not so curved that he cannot see the light at the end. (See Figure 13-3.) Increase the degree of curve. Finally put a sharp bend into the tunnel and send him into the tunnel from a distance. Then make the tunnel into an S bend. This is sometimes hard to do with a fifteen-foot tunnel.

Figure 13-1. Tunnel opening appears large with a straight on approach.

Figure 13-2. Tunnel opening looks narrower with an angled approach.

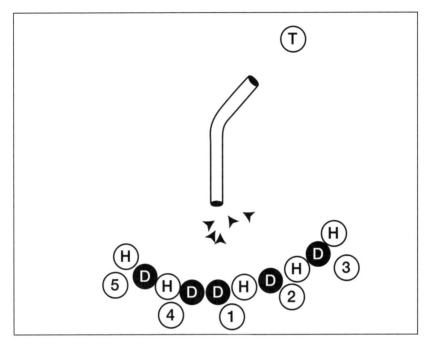

Figure 13-3. Teach your dog to find the tunnel entrance.
Send him from the various angles designated by the numbers 1–5.

Step 3

Send him into the tunnel when you are both moving forward. Keep him on leash so that if he tries to run by the entrance you can check him. At this stage of his training, he should feel comfortable running next to you, on both your right and left sides. Start about ten feet from the tunnel with him on your left. Tell him, "Go tunnel," give a signal, and start running toward the tunnel. Do not run directly at the tunnel entrance. (See Figure 13-4.) If you do, you will probably force your dog away from it. Remember how you ran off to the side of the jump uprights? Your approach line will be to the side of the tunnel. If he commits to the tunnel, simply let the leash drop. If he tries to run past the tunnel entrance, use your leash to check him, and then use it to guide him into the tunnel. If he is successful, repeat this several times, and then begin again with him on your right. Next, start running toward the tunnel from different angles. Remove the leash.

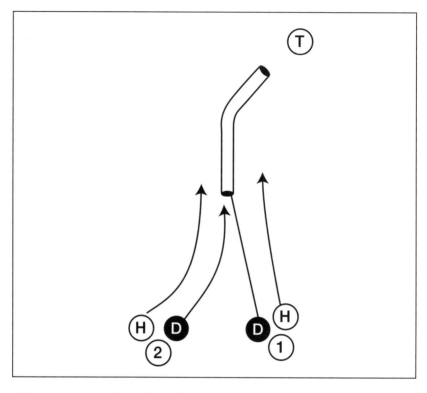

Figure 13-4. Run with your dog on both your left and your right toward the tunnel. Do not run directly at the tunnel entrance.

Step 4

Remove the target. After your dog has run through the tunnel, call him to you and reward him.

Tunnel Commitment

You want your dog to commit to running through the tunnel so that even if you hesitate in front of it while running a course, he will still go through. When I send my dog to get a dumbbell, I know he will go and get it. With the training he has received, he is committed to retrieving. I believe my dog should have that same commitment to go through the tunnel. When I know my dog understands his job on retrieve, I put him back on leash. I throw the dumbbell and send him for it. As he leaves my side, I apply tension to the leash so he has to drag me out in order to reach the dumbbell. As soon as he picks it up, I break the exercise and reward him. I find this actually makes for a stronger retrieve. When I know my dog understands to run through the tunnel, I use a similar approach. I put my dog back on leash. I then give him the command to go through the tunnel, and as he moves toward it, I apply tension to the leash. (See Figure 13-5.) If he pulls me toward the tunnel, I really pour on the praise and give him lots of encouragement. The moment he enters the tunnel, I release the leash and greet him at the other end with a big reward. However, if he hesitates, I repeat the command and encourage him to move forward. I may even give a light pop on the leash to convince him that he has no option. What I do at this point depends on the type of dog I am training. I test my dog's commitment to running through the tunnel periodically. I need to know that he is committed to going through it, no matter what.

Figure 13-5. Tunnel commitment. Dog drags handler to tunnel entrance.

Goal: To Include the Tunnel in a Sequence of Jumps

Step 1

Most of the time when you run an agility course, some other obstacle precedes the tunnel. If you have reached the point in your training where your dog is jumping over a series of jumps, you should place a jump in front of the tunnel. Remember that your dog will be building up speed when he jumps. Running into the tunnel after jumping a jump is a lot different than running into the tunnel off the start line. When jumping, a dog is lifting off. When he goes into the tunnel, he may need to crouch. This takes two different skills, so be patient. Begin this exercise with a straight tunnel so that the entrance is bright, not dark. Start with one jump in front of the tunnel and place your motivator just beyond the exit. Tell your dog, "Go jump. Go tunnel. OK, get it." When your dog can successfully sail over a jump and then dive into the tunnel, you can put a bend in the tunnel.

Step 2

Add a jump for him to take upon exiting the tunnel. Now he will have to look ahead to see what obstacle comes next. Put a bend to the right in the tunnel, to slow your dog down. Add a single bar jump about eighteen feet beyond the tunnel exit. Position your motivator beyond that jump. (See Figure 13-6.) Tell your dog, "Go jump. Go tunnel. Go jump. OK, get it." Run with him as he takes the jump, runs through the tunnel, and jumps the second jump. In this exercise, you will stay on the same side of the dog throughout the sequence. After several repetitions bend the tunnel to the left and run with your dog on your right. Once he is performing this exercise correctly, you can remove the target. Put him on a schedule of random reinforcement.

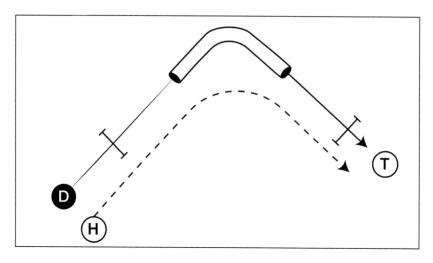

Figure 13-6. Jump, tunnel, jump. You can save time by cutting across from the tunnel entrance straight to the exit.

Step 3

Bend the tunnel to the right. Place the jump after the tunnel to the right of the exit. Your dog will have to make a 90-degree turn when he comes out of the tunnel. While your dog is in the tunnel, run and position yourself to the right of the tunnel exit, facing the exit. As your dog emerges, say, "Come" and turn to the right to face the jump. Send him over the jump. Repeat with the tunnel bent to the left and the jump to the left of the tunnel exit.

Step 4

Place a jump in front of the tunnel exit and another to the right of the tunnel, as you did in the previous exercise. (See Figure 13-7.) You will now be able to practice a "call-off" as your dog comes out of the tunnel. He will see the jump that is in front of the tunnel exit and will want to take it. One time have him take that jump, and the next time have him turn and take the jump to the side.

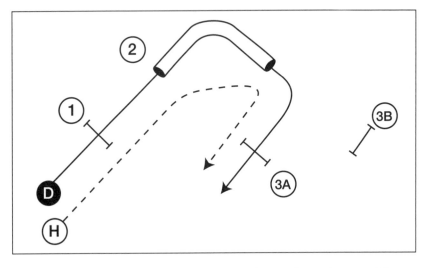

Figure 13-7. Practice a "call-off" coming out of the tunnel. One time turn right and have your dog jump obstacle 3A. The next time have him take 3B.

Step 5

Add two jumps before the tunnel. The greater number of jumps your dog takes before reaching the tunnel, the faster he is likely to be moving. He may miss the tunnel entrance when he is working at greater speed.

> **Remember, like the tire jump, the tunnel can frame an obstacle at its exit. That obstacle may not always be the obstacle you wish your dog to take next.**

Goal: To Introduce a Blind Side Switch

Many agility courses are set up so that the handler can switch sides at the tunnel. When the dog is in the tunnel, he cannot see you make the side switch. For this reason, it is called a blind side switch.

There are two types of side switches. Depending on your dog's training and his speed, the switch might occur at the tunnel entrance, which is called a "cross behind." You are crossing behind your dog's path. A "cross in front" would take place at the tunnel exit. Handlers of slow dogs rarely need to cross behind at any point on the course. A "cross behind" can cause your dog to slow down when he looks back to see what he might be missing. This could also lead to a refusal at the next obstacle. He might miss it because he is so busy looking to see what you are up to. In addition, if your dog starts to slow up as you make a "cross behind," it is possible you might actually collide with each other. So first, teach him a "cross in front," because you will definitely need one in competition.

Step 1: "Cross in Front"

Set up the tunnel with a sharp bend to the left. The bend should slow your dog down, allowing you time to get into position. Place a single bar jump both before and after the tunnel. Begin with your dog on your right side. Tell him, "Go jump. Go tunnel," and as he enters the tunnel continue running toward the exit, keeping the tunnel (obstacle 2) on your right. Cross in front of the tunnel exit, and pivot in toward the tunnel. Continue turning until you are facing (obstacle 3). As your dog emerges from the tunnel, he will be on your left. Before he reaches the end of the tunnel, he should hear you saying, "Go jump." You need to let him know what obstacle is coming next. In addition, he will also realize you are no longer on the same side, from the direction of your voice. As your dog exits from the tunnel, begin to run in the direction of obstacle 3, giving him a hand signal with your left arm. (See Figure 13-8.) It may take a little practice for both of you to get it right. For the

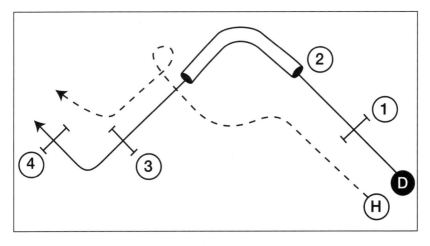

Figure 13-8. "Cross in front" at tunnel. With your dog on your left after the tunnel it will be easy to turn him right to take obstacle 4.

first time, you are being asked to do something other than run in a fairly straight line. There is no exercise in obedience that requires the type of footwork needed for a "cross in front." It takes some getting used to. You will quickly find out how easy it is to trip over your own two feet. You do not even need a dancing partner. Practice this cross several times until you get a feel for what you are doing. Your dog needs to understand that you may suddenly reappear on the opposite side from where he last saw you.

Step 2: "Cross in Front"

Bend the tunnel to the right, and run with your dog on your left. This time, when you switch sides at the tunnel exit, your dog will end up on your right. Always pass in front of the exit and turn toward the tunnel. You should be watching for your dog to come out and not have your back to the tunnel.

Step 1: "Cross Behind"

Now comes the tricky part. You are going to try a "cross behind." You will do this only if you have a dog that is working ahead of you. The footwork for the "cross behind" is much easier than for the "cross in front." Set the tunnel up with a bend to the right, with a jump before and after it. Run with your dog on your right. Send him over the jump and into the tunnel. As he commits to the tunnel, cross to the right side of the tunnel. With the tunnel on your left, run toward the tunnel exit but do not pass in front of it. Face the second jump. Before your dog exits the tunnel, tell him, "Go jump." As he appears at the tunnel exit, he will be on your left. Signal toward the jump and start running forward. Send him over the jump and then reward him. (See Figure 13-9.) Practice this sequence several times and then change the tunnel so that the bend is to the left.

Step 2: "Cross Behind"

Run with your dog on your left. As your dog commits to the tunnel, cross to the left side. Continue running to the tunnel exit with the tunnel on your right. When your dog emerges from the tunnel, he will be on your right.

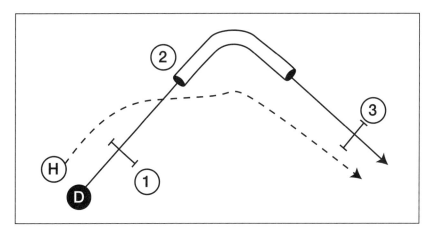

Figure 13-9. A "cross behind" takes place at the tunnel entrance.

Continue to work on both the "cross behind" and the "cross in front." Also, practice sending your dog through the tunnel without switching sides. You do not want him to think that you will switch sides every time he is in a tunnel.

If your dog is slow going into the tunnel, try throwing a motivator to land just beyond the tunnel exit as he emerges from the tunnel. You may even need to go back to placing a target beyond the jump that follows the tunnel. To speed up one of my dogs going through the tunnel, I placed a soccer ball right inside the tunnel exit. This was her favorite toy, and she would dash through the tunnel to hit it with her nose and chase it out of the tunnel. Because the ball rolled so easily, she did not have to slow down when she reached it. When I set up a course for her to run, the soccer ball would be in the tunnel exit but invisible to her while on the course.

Most dogs seem to like the tunnels so well that they will choose to take them over many of the other obstacles on the course. This is known as a "tunnel-suck" and a favorite trap set by judges. Once a dog is successfully running through the open tunnel, you can introduce the chute tunnel.

The Collapsed Tunnel

The collapsed tunnel presents more problems to small dogs than large due to the size of the dog having to push through the chute. A dog needs to have momentum to get out of the chute. If you happen to be running in an outdoor trial when it is raining, the cloth can become extremely heavy. Some dogs are intimidated by the feel of the material on their backs. However, dogs that sleep in bed, under the covers, should have no problem with the chute.

A word of caution when using a collapsed tunnel! The cloth portion of the chute cannot be anchored like the pipe tunnel. You must take great care that the chute tunnel is not placed near another obstacle, wall, fence, tree, or anything the dog could run into while he is inside the chute. He will be unable to see a hazard.

NADAC is using an eight-foot chute. This presents much less of a challenge for small dogs. I prefer to use an eight-foot chute for training because a dog can get through it faster and it makes the training of this exercise that much easier. However, if you train with an eight-foot chute, be sure to practice with a twelve-foot one before running your dog in AKC and USDAA competition.

Goal: To Send Your Dog Through the Collapsed Tunnel

Step 1

Introduce your dog to the barrel by calling him through it, and then sending him through it, as you did when introducing the pipe tunnel.

Step 2

Attach the chute to the barrel. Sit your dog in front of the end of the chute. If you have a training partner, have her raise the upper layer of the chute higher than your dog's head. Go to the barrel end and call your dog through the chute. If you do not have a training partner, place your dog's motivator several feet in front of the barrel. You will have to hold up the upper layer of the chute as you send your dog through the chute and out through the barrel. You teach your dog to run through the collapsed tunnel in reverse. He will be going from the unknown into the known. The barrel will appear more like the exit of an open tunnel when he enters the chute; therefore he should feel more comfortable going in that direction.

Step 3

Gradually lower the cloth of the chute so it is touching your dog's back as he runs through it to the barrel. Finally, as he enters the chute, drop the upper layer so he has to push to get to the other end.

Step 4

When he is running confidently through the chute, in reverse, it is time to send him through the barrel and into the chute. If you have a training partner, have her go to the end of the chute and hold up the cloth so your dog can see a little daylight at the end. If you are training by yourself, sit your dog in front of the barrel and go to the end of the chute. You will raise up the cloth so your dog can see daylight. Tell him, "Go tunnel," and give him lots of praise when he reaches you. When he is confidently pushing through the tunnel, you can move to Step 5.

Step 5

Run with your dog to the collapsed tunnel entrance. While he is inside the chute, run to the end and encourage him to chase you as he comes out of the tunnel. Begin with him on your left, and then repeat the exercise with him on your right. You want your dog to come bursting out of the chute, because a dog that goes through slowly is more likely to get trapped in the cloth. This might be a good time to throw his motivator, or a food tube, just as his head emerges from the chute.

Goal: To Include the Collapsed Tunnel in a Sequence of Jumps

Step 1

Introduce the jumps before and after the chute tunnel, like you did with the pipe tunnel. Obviously, you cannot put a bend in the collapsed tunnel. Position the jump after the chute at least twenty feet from the exit, in the beginning. (See Figure 13-10.) Remember that your dog will be momentarily blind as he exits the chute and may not see the jump if it is too close to the exit.

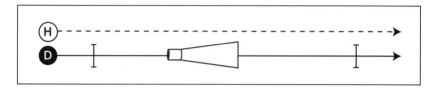

Figure 13-10. Introduce the chute tunnel into a jumping sequence.

Step 2

Place a jump at a 90-degree angle to the right of the exit of the chute. Send your dog through the chute on your left and run to the end. When your dog emerges, say, "Come," and turn right, sending your dog over the jump. Repeat, turning your dog to the left after the chute and sending him over a jump.

Step 3

Practice a "call-off" by setting up two jumps, one placed in front of the chute and the other to the right or the left of the exit at a 90-degree angle

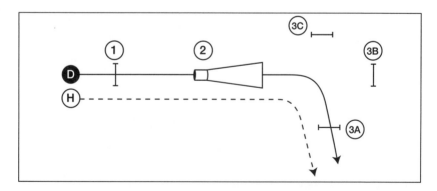

Figure 13-11. Practice a "call-off" coming out of the chute. One time turn right and have your dog jump obstacle 3A. The next time have him take 3B as you did in Figure 13-7. Finally, run with him on your right, turn left, and have him take 3C.

to the chute. Alternate by having your dog take the jump in front of the chute exit or turn to take the jump on the side. (See Figure 13-11.)

Goal: To Introduce a "Cross in Front" and a "Cross Behind" at the Chute Tunnel

Step 1: "Cross in Front"

Place a jump at a 90-degree angle to the right of the chute exit. Run with your dog on your right, sending him over a jump and into the collapsed tunnel. Run past the chute, and cross in front of the exit while your dog is inside. Encourage your dog as he passes through the chute so that he hears which side you are on. As he exits, say, "Come." Turn right and say, "Go jump," signal with your left arm, and run with him toward the jump. (See Figure 13-12.) He will be on your left when he exits the collapsed tunnel. After several repetitions, move the jump to the opposite side of the tunnel exit. Repeat the exercise by running with your dog on your left. When you cross in front at the chute exit, you will turn left when your dog emerges from the chute and send him over the jump from your right.

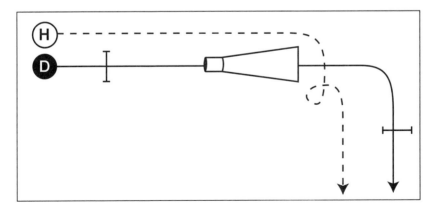

Figure 13-12. A "cross in front" at the chute.

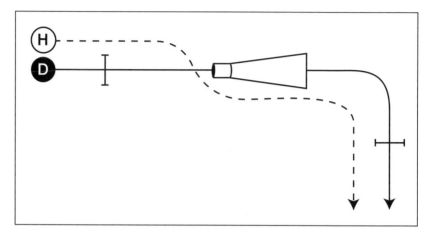

Figure 13-13. A "cross behind" at the chute.

Step 2: "Cross Behind"

Run with your dog on your right and send him over the jump and into the collapsed tunnel. Cross behind the barrel to the right side and run to the end of the chute. You need to let your dog know you are no longer on his same side. Give him verbal encouragement while he is in the chute so that when he exits he will know where you are. Turn him to the right at the exit of the chute and send him over the jump. (See Figure 13-13.)

Step 3

Add another jump before and after the collapsed tunnel.

If you intend to run your dog at outdoor trials, now is the time to teach him to run through a wet chute. Turn on the hose and spray the cloth with water. Send your dog through a couple of times. Eventually really soak the cloth with water. One day you may have to run your dog during a downpour, and he needs to have experience with a wet, heavy chute.

Tunnel Troubles

In obedience, there are problem areas associated with almost every exercise. The same holds true for agility. If you know where problems are likely to occur, it is easier to deal with them before they become ingrained in your dog.

Some dogs go into the tunnel and immediately turn around and come back out the entrance instead of continuing to the exit. This often occurs when you start doing a "cross behind." Your dog senses you are changing direction and comes back out to see where you are going. Another reason is that you call him too early after he gets into the tunnel. If he is turning around and coming out of the tunnel, try keeping silent as you run toward the exit. Only start calling him when you think he has passed the halfway point. Dogs tend to do less turning around once they have had experience in running through tunnels. Some dogs make a game out of going in and then popping out again. If it happens with the pipe tunnel, have your agility partner turn the entrance end of the tunnel over into the ground the moment your dog enters. This will not affect him if he continues forward, but if he turns around to come back out, he will not be able to do so. This is a form of correction but not one that should upset the dog.

Another problem is also handler-induced. The handler runs with the dog right up to the tunnel entrance and stops dead. The dog, paying attention to the handler, stops too and incurs a refusal. Sometimes a tunnel is in a tight C configuration with the entrance and exit very close together. The handler stops because there is no place to run once she reaches the tunnel. If, instead, the handler reduces her speed on the approach to the tunnel, she can stop after the dog has entered. I teach tunnel commitment as a means of preventing this problem.

Occasionally a dog will enter a tunnel and stay there. If you go to one end of the tunnel to try to entice him out, he will turn and go toward the other end. One Christmas I was boarding a dog that had this problem. The owner asked if I could try to eliminate it while the dog was staying with me. I knew a leash would be of no help because, if you grabbed hold of the leash, it would cause the dog to turn around in the tunnel and he would come out the way he went in. I tried to get "Rip" to run through the tunnel by using his motivator, but he was too smart for that. I was dealing with a dog that was tough and headstrong. I did not want to wait on him all day. I grabbed a bar off a jump and banged it on the top of the tunnel, and the dog came out of the tunnel like a shot from a cannon. I gave him lots of praise and acted as though I had nothing to do with what had happened. We worked on some other equipment successfully, and then we went back and did the tunnel again. This time I was ready with the bar. As I heard Rip start to slow down, I rapped on the top of the tunnel, and out he came. It did not take many repetitions until he was racing through the tunnel with no hesitation. If a dog cannot see you make a correction, it is often extremely effective. However, you would never do this with a noise-sensitive dog or a dog that did not thoroughly understand the tunnel exercise. You would not try this with a dog in the chute tunnel because the bar would actually hit the dog. Pipe tunnels have wire to hold the fabric off the dog's back.

Some dogs like to anoint the inside of the tunnel when they are going through it. This is a serious problem both for the owner of the dog who is doing the dirty deed and for other dogs that have to go into the tunnel afterward. Occasionally at a trial you will see a dog that has been working well up to the tunnel refuse to go in. The dog will have a revolted expression on his face. Some dogs are so fastidious that they will not enter a tunnel that has been fouled. If you own a dog that likes to mark in a tunnel, the bar bang might be the answer to get him over this nasty habit. You would think that a dog would have to stop to mark, but I have actually seen a dog come out of the tunnel on three legs, running and marking at the same time.

A friend of mine told me of the time her Border Collie learned how to go through the chute tunnel. Her dog had quickly caught on to running through the open tunnel but was hesitant to enter the chute. By chance, this Border Collie was in line behind a small, fuzzy dog that loved to race through the chute. Small, fuzzy dogs fascinated the Border Collie, so when the little dog disappeared into the barrel, the Border Collie was anxious to follow. A few times chasing after the little dog was all it took to teach one Border Collie to look forward to entering the chute. Sometimes, if you have a dog that is reluctant to go into the chute, you might consider sending your dog to follow a canine buddy.

Chapter 14

Staying on Top of Things

Table commands are usually "table," "bench," and "get on."

The pause table is probably the easiest obstacle to teach in all of agility. However, more dogs than you would expect incur one or more penalties at this obstacle in competition. The reason for this is that many handlers consider the table such an easy obstacle that they never take the time to teach it properly. I equate pause table training with teaching the "down stay." Many obedience handlers never bother to properly teach their dogs the "down stay" exercise either. They just tell the dog, "stay" without really making sure the dog understands what is expected of him. The "down stay," like the pause table, is an easy exercise. However, a number of dogs fail both on a regular basis.

There are several reasons why a dog incurs penalties at the pause table. He may refuse to get up on the table. He may stop in front of it or jump on from the back side of the table, thereby incurring a refusal. He may jump on it and then slide off. Many dogs refuse to sit or lie down on the table or do not hold position for the count of five. It never ceases to amaze me watching the gyrations some handlers have to go through to get their dogs to "sit" or "down" on the table and then try to keep them there. A few handlers actually kneel on the ground and act as if they are paying homage at the altar. Some dogs anticipate the table count and leave the table before the handler calls them. The table should not be much of a challenge if it is trained correctly from the beginning. Before you attempt to teach the table, review teaching the "sit," "down," and "stay" in Chapter 4.

Instructions on how to make a table can be found in Appendix B. If you do not want to make anything as elaborate, you can make a pause "box" out of 2 × 4s standing on edge supporting a three-foot square top.

Goal: To Teach Your Dog to Get on the Table

In AKC competition there are only three table heights. Although you may find it impossible to set the table lower than eight inches, which is the table height used for small breeds, most little dogs are at a distinct advantage on this exercise. Even an eight-inch table is considerably lower than the couch or bed they jump on and off all day long! For dogs that require a table higher than eight inches, to start your training set the table lower than your dog is going to face in competition.

Step 1

Put your dog on leash. Walk him up to the table and pat the top of the table as you say, "Go table." Encourage him to jump on the table, and then praise and reward him. Do not make him "sit" or "down" on the table, but hold on to his leash or collar to prevent him from immediately getting off. Finally, give him his release word and allow him to get off the table. Repeat this several times, moving with your dog on both your left and your right.

Step 2

Place his motivator toward the back of the tabletop. You want your dog to get all the way onto the table. Depending on where you position his motivator, he might be able to reach it while his feet remain on the ground. If you use food and are concerned about having your dog sniffing the tabletop once the food is removed, either utilize a food tube or place a margarine tub lid on the table and lay the food on it. With your dog about ten feet from the table and still on leash say, "Look, go table." Run with him toward the table, and have him jump up on it. Praise him, but do not allow him to get off the table for several seconds. He may sit, lie down, or stand on the table. You can tell him, "Wait" or "Stay" once he is on it. It is your job to keep him on the table. Repeat this exercise several times by running with him on both your left and your right.

Step 3

Remove the leash and send your dog ahead of you onto the table. Do not allow him to leave the table without a release word. After several repetitions remove the target and reward him from your hand once he is up on the table. Occasionally, put his motivator back on the table to give him a reason to hurry.

Step 4

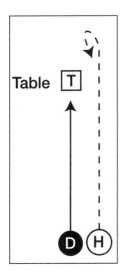

Table [T]

Figure 14-1. Handler runs past table, and then turns around. Dog must stay on table.

Put your dog back on leash. Run with him toward the table so that the table is to your left. As he lands on it, say, "Stay" or "Wait" as you continue to run. Come to a stop and turn around once you have gone a couple of feet beyond the back edge of the table. (See Figure 14-1.) If your dog tries to follow you, use your leash to prevent him from getting off the table or use it to make him jump back on. Praise and reward him. Do several repetitions with your dog running on both your left and your right. Next, take the leash off and run with him to the table. As he jumps on it, remind him to "stay" or "wait" and continue running until you are several feet past the table. If he stays on the table, return to him and praise and reward him. If he gets off the table, catch hold of his collar and make him get back on. If you have to do this, do not reward him—only praise him once he is back on the table. Repeat this exercise several times until he never considers getting off the table until he hears his release word.

Step 5

Put him back on leash. Now you are going to test his understanding of the exercise. Send and run with him toward the table. Continue past the table, and then stop and apply tension to the leash. If he jumps off, verbally let him know he is wrong. Then use your leash to get him back onto the table. Praise him once he is up there. If he resists the tension and stays on the table, then return to him and reward and praise him.

Goal: To Call Your Dog onto the Table

Step 1

Leave him on a "sit stay" about fifteen feet from the table. Lead out and position yourself on the opposite side of the table. Tell him, "Come, table" and have him run and jump on the table in a similar manner to how he would perform the recall. If he stays on the table, praise and reward him. Gradually position yourself farther from the table as you call him to get on it. As he jumps onto the table, take one quick step toward him as a reminder to stop and not to continue toward you. You may have used a similar technique when you taught him the drop-on-recall to prevent him from traveling forward on the "down" and remain at a distance from you. He must learn to stay on the table once he is up on it, just as he learned to stay on the down-on-recall. Return to him, and praise and reward him. This exercise teaches a fast dog to dig in and stick on the table.

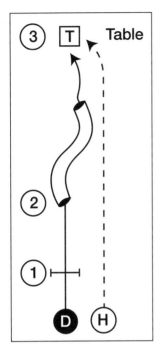

Figure 14-2.
Jump, tunnel, table.

Step 2

Place a jump about fifteen feet in front of the table. Run with him and have him take the jump and then get on the table. When he takes a jump first, he is likely to approach the table at greater speed and may slide off it. Substitute the jump with the tunnel. Have him do *jump, tunnel, table,* and then *tunnel, jump, table.* (See Figure 14-2.)

Goal: Table Commitment

You want your dog to commit to getting on the table so that even if you should happen to hesitate in front of it while running a course, he will still get on. You teach this in the same way as you would teach tunnel commitment. (See Chapter 13.) Put your dog back on leash. Give him the command to go to the table, and as he moves toward it, apply tension to the leash. If he pulls you toward the table, really pour on the praise and give him lots of encouragement. However, if he hesitates as he feels tension on the leash, repeat the command and encourage him to move forward. You may even give a light pop forward with the leash to convince him that he must go and get on the table. Test your dog's commitment to running to the table periodically in the early stages of table training. You need to know that he is committed to getting on the table, once he has been told to do so.

Goal: To Have Your Dog "Sit" and "Down" on the Table

Until your dog can "sit" and "down" on command next to you on both your right and left sides, and in front of you, there is no point in trying to have him do those same commands on the table.

Step 1

Put your dog back on leash. Send him to the table as you did in Step 2 when you first introduced him to it. Do not place his motivator on the table. The moment he lands on the table, tell him, "Down." Then if he does not immediately assume the "down" position, catch hold of his collar, and make him lie down. Do not turn into one of those handlers who go through all kinds of gyrations to get their dogs down. Keep in mind that seconds count in agility, and you want your dog to respond to the command quickly. The moment he lies down, praise and reward him with food or a toy. Release him and allow him to get off the table. Do several repetitions with him on both your left and your right. One problem that often occurs with dogs trained in obedience is that they respond so quickly once you give the command, that they lie down before they are on the table. This has happened to me on more than one occasion. Several times I gave my "down" command prematurely, and my dog dropped at the base of the table!

Step 2

Repeat the exercise, but have him sit rather than lie down on the table. If he goes into the "down," make him sit up by pulling gently up on the leash. Remember that you have recently been practicing "lie down" on the table, so it is understandable if he becomes confused when you tell him to sit. Eventually you will need to practice the "sit up from the down" since he may become confused and assume the wrong position in competition. In both AKC and UKC agility trials, the judge is the one who decides whether the dog is to do a "sit" or "down" on the pause table.

Step 3

Mix it up by sometimes having your dog "sit," sometimes having him "down," and often only having him get up on the table and stay there, as he did in the beginning.

Step 4

Apply tension to the leash when he is in both the "sit" and "down" on the table. He must learn to wait until you release him from the position he has assumed. (See Figures 14-3 and 14-4.)

Figure 14-3. Testing the dog to see if he will remain staying on the pause table.

Figure 14-4. Testing the dog to see if he will remain lying down on the table.

Step 5

Introduce a "cross in front" at the table. This is one of the places where you will often find it necessary to use this technique. Once your dog has assumed the "sit" or "down" position, tell him, "Stay" and then cross to the other side of the table. (See Figure 14-5 to see how to do a "cross in front" at the table.)

Goal: To Call Your Dog off the Table and Send Him to Another Obstacle

Step 1

Set up the sequence of *jump, tunnel, table,* which you will now have your dog run in reverse. Put him on leash and have him get on the table. The first couple of times you call him off the table, you will only have him run through the tunnel; therefore lay the jump bars on the ground. Because you have been making your dog stay on the table, he may be reluctant to leave it at first. The leash will assist you in getting him to leave the table if needed. Walk about five feet toward the tunnel and then turn to face your dog, holding your leash in your left hand with some slack in the leash. As you tell your dog, "Go tunnel," pivot to your right so that your dog and the tunnel will be positioned on your left. If he does not respond by immediately jumping off the table, the leash will tighten as you move toward the tunnel, thereby giving him a slight correction. As he starts into the tunnel, let go of the leash and let it drag behind him. Meet him at the other end, and reward and praise him. Repeat by leaving him on the table while you hold the leash in your right hand. This time, turn to your left when you call him. This will position him and the tunnel on your right side. Once he figures out that he must jump off the table when commanded, you can remove the leash and then include the jump after the tunnel. Switch the jump and the tunnel so that when he leaves the table, he takes a jump first before he goes through the tunnel. Then as he emerges from the tunnel, throw his motivator as a reward.

Step 2

If you need to speed him up getting off the table, occasionally tell him to come, and then throw his motivator for him to chase without sending him over or through any obstacles.

Step 3

Send him to the table by sending him over the jump and through the tunnel. Have him sit or lie down on the table, and then call him back through the tunnel and over the jump. He will be running on one side of you on the way out and the other side on the way back. Do not always run all the way up to the table, but hang back closer to the tunnel exit/entrance. You can switch the tunnel and jump so that when he leaves the table he takes the jump and then the tunnel.

Step 4

With the same setup, start with him on your left by sending him over the jump, through the tunnel, and onto the table. Go up to the table, and "cross in front" to the other side so that he will be on your left once more. Call him off the table and send him back through the tunnel and over the jump. (See Figure 14-5.) Repeat this by having him run on your right.

Once your dog is comfortable with these pause table exercises, add additional jumps including the tire. Add obstacles after the table that may encourage him to keep on going rather than stop on top of the

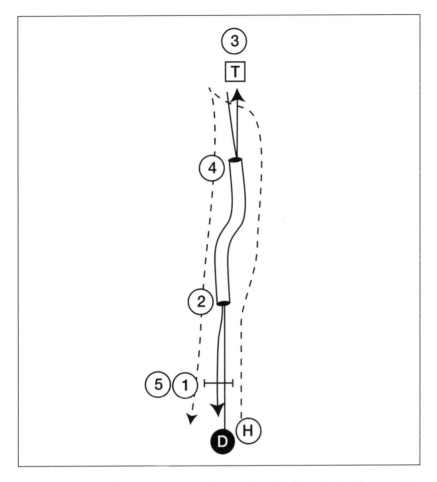

Figure 14-5. Run with your dog on your left up to the table. "Cross in front" at the table, and then run with him on your left on your return.

table. (See Figure 14-6.) When you are no longer reversing direction after the dog is on the table, you can include the chute tunnel and spread jumps. Remember that these obstacles can be taken only in one direction. Finally, raise the height of the table to competition height.

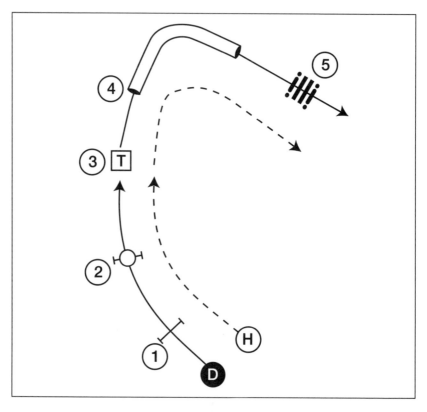

Figure 14-6. Because most dogs like to run through tunnels, placing the tunnel after the table may encourage your dog to keep on going, rather than stop on the table.

Table Torment

You may find yourself facing the following table problems, and these are some solutions for dealing with them.

If your dog consistently runs past the table, put him back on leash and use it to check him the moment he starts to pass it by. If you believe he is afraid of the table, place a motivator on it for an added incentive to get onto the table.

If your dog runs up to the table and then stops his forward motion and fails to get up on it, this is a similar problem to a dog that runs up to the tunnel and stops dead at the entrance. You may be coming to an abrupt stop and your dog is responding accordingly. As you approach the table with your dog, try slowing down and holding back rather than coming to a complete stop. Only cease your forward motion once your dog is actually on the table. In addition to changing your handling of this exercise, work on table commitment.

Sometimes you see a dog run under the table. This is particularly true at outside shows in hot weather. When dogs are hot, they will seek shade, and they most likely have already learned that they can always find shade under a table. If you have a dog that likes to go under the table, surround the base with chicken wire chutes to prevent him from doing so. Also, place some object or the table legs themselves under the table. A dog that stops to look at an object lying under the table at a trial will earn a refusal. If the table is located in the center of the course, the additional table legs occasionally are left underneath it to lessen the time needed to change jump heights. I have watched dog after dog incur table faults by checking out legs stored underneath the table when they are running a course.

A problem that often occurs when running a fast dog is that he gets on the table at such speed that he slides right off it. This is particularly true at an outdoor trial when it is damp out. If you have a fast dog, you may wish to practice soaking the table with water so that he learns to grip the surface and hold on. Another thing you can do is place plastic wrap on the table surface so he is more careful as he gets on that he does not slide off again. Put wrap on the table and then call him to the table while you stand at some distance on the opposite side. Lay several chicken wire chutes between the table and the point where you are standing so that if he slides off the table he will run into the wire. If you have problems with him only sliding off in competition, give him the command "easy" as he approaches the table.

When the table is wet from dew or rain at an outside show, many dogs are reluctant to assume a "down" position. At home, practice having your dog lie down on a wet table. At a trial, make him lie down in the wet grass several times before your run, and insist that he lie down quickly, with his elbows on the ground.

Chapter 15

Comprehending Contacts

Why do some of the agility obstacles have a contact zone? For one reason—safety! By requiring a dog to touch a contact zone, he will have to get on and leave the obstacle in a safe manner. You do not want a dog leaping high up onto the narrow boards of the dog walk and seesaw because it would be hard for him to maintain balance and he could possibly fall off. You do not want him jumping off the peak of the A-frame, the top of the dog walk, nor the end of the seesaw as he starts to descend. By doing so he could be injured. Once a dog reaches the area of the down contact zone, he is close enough to the ground that he will be less likely to get hurt should he jump off without waiting to be released by his handler.

Contact zones are always painted a different color than the body of the equipment. Traditionally, the color used is yellow, but the color of the zone may be any color as long as it contrasts with the rest of the equipment. This allows the judge to see whether a dog is properly in the zone when getting on or off. The contact zone for AKC trials is forty-two inches up from the end of all ramps. USDAA and NADAC use forty-two inches for the A-frame and thirty-six inches for the dog walk, seesaw, and crossover. The crossover is seldom seen on an agility course because it takes up so much space.

If you were to ask five successful agility trainers how they teach the contacts, the requirement they are most likely to have in common is that the dog must not leave the contact obstacle without permission of the handler. Where you will not find agreement is on exactly where and how the dog should stop. Some trainers train a dog to stop with the dog's two rear feet on the obstacle and the two front paws on the ground. Others want the dog to stop completely on the ramp. Some trainers have the dog lie down or sit at the bottom of the ramp. There is no right or wrong way, just as long as the dog stops and you insist that he does it the same way every time. There are some minor drawbacks no matter which way you have the dog stop. If you want a dog to stop with all four feet on the ramp, there is always the possibility that he may begin to stop farther and farther up the ramp until he stops out of the contact zone altogether. You will then lose time while you encourage him to move into the contact area so that you can allow him to leave the obstacle without incurring a penalty. If you ask the dog to stop with two feet on and two feet off the ramp, there is the possibility that your dog may simply keep on going when running a course. If you want your dog to assume a "sit" or "down" position at the end of the contact, this may add time to your run. However, a blown contact is failure to perform, so you are better off losing a few seconds by having him take his time than by having him leave the contact prematurely.

A dog that is looking down when he is descending the ramp is far less likely to jump off the obstacle than the dog who is looking ahead to see what obstacle comes next. (See Figure 15-1.) When a dog is looking ahead, he is not thinking about the obstacle on which he is performing at that moment. Many people who get into agility do not realize just how important it is to insist that the dog remain on the contact—that is, until he has already formed the bad habit of leaving on his own. It is far more difficult to retrain your dog to wait for your release than it is to teach him to remain on the contact in the first place. Some exhibitors, particularly those with slow dogs, see no reason to teach their dogs to perform in this manner. They fear that they may slow their dogs down even more by being so demanding. However, many dogs pick up speed as they become more confident in agility. With added speed, they begin to ignore contacts! When I got into the sport, I was guilty of not requiring my two oldest dogs to remain in the contact zone until released because they were not speedy. However, I was careful to make sure my two young dogs froze on the contacts. As my older dogs became more comfortable in agility, their speed increased. Today, these are the dogs that incur penalties on the contact obstacles rather than my younger dogs, which I took time to train correctly from the beginning.

Figure 15-1. Dog looking down as he descends the A-frame.

You should start your contact obstacle training with the A-frame. This obstacle is considerably wider than the dog walk or seesaw, and in addition, it can be set at a low angle, making it a much safer obstacle to use initially. Many dogs have never learned how to control their rear ends, and the additional width of the A-frame makes it less likely that they will slip off this obstacle. Falling off the narrower dog walk or the seesaw could make your dog fearful of the contact obstacles and end a career in agility before it ever begins. Obedience dogs trained to "heel" backward are at an advantage here, because they have already learned how to control their rear ends. However, many trainers do not bother to teach this skill to their dogs. If your dog appears to have no idea of where his rear end belongs, you should consider teaching him to walk between the rungs of an extension ladder. This is a simple way of teaching a dog how to control his rear end while on the ground, rather than up in the air. Many people do not own an extension ladder, but you may find a neighbor willing to lend or rent one to you for a few days while you teach your dog to think about where he places his rear feet. Lay the ladder on the ground and then have your dog step over the rungs of the ladder while you walk alongside him, as you might on the dog walk. Walk with him while you are on both the right and the left of the ladder.

On ramps in buildings, there are handrails for people to hold on to for security. Contact obstacle ramps provide no such security for your dog. However, you can place your traffic cones at the start and end of the ramp to give your dog something to focus on. (See Figure 15-2.) Your dog is used to passing between uprights of jumps, so by placing cones or even jump uprights at the start and end of the contact obstacle, you can give him an added sense of security in the beginning.

Before teaching your dog any contact obstacle, first consider where you want him to stop on the contact. If you normally use a toy as a target, this may present a problem. Many dogs are used to picking up their toys and then running off with them, which might encourage your dog to leave the contact prematurely. Most trainers recommend using food as the target for the contact obstacles. If you use food, where should you place it? If you are going to require your dog to have two feet on and two feet off the ramp, then you will need to place the target where he cannot

Figure 15-2. Using traffic cones to mark the beginning and end of the ramp.

touch the food until he has reached the required position. If you are placing the food on the ground, you can use a food tube or place the food on the lid of a margarine tub. This is one instance when you do not want to raise the food up off the ground since you want your dog's head to be held low when coming down the ramp. You also want him to see the target easily. The distance you place the target from the bottom of the ramp is based on the size of your dog. You will need to place the target farther from the ramp if you have a large dog than a small one. A large dog can reach farther than a small one, and you want your dog's front feet to be on the ground before he gets to eat the food. A large dog could remain on the ramp and still reach the food if it is placed too close to the ramp. If you want your dog to stop on the ramp itself, then no matter the size of your dog, place the food near the end of the ramp. Alternatively, you can place the food on the lid of a margarine tub so that the ramp itself does not become contaminated with food.

Most trainers agree that you should teach the dog what is required of him on the down ramp of the contact obstacle before you introduce him to the entire obstacle. If you elect to do this, you will need to lift him onto the down ramp. This is not always easy if you own a large or heavy dog. If you are physically unable to lift your dog onto the obstacle, you can position the pause table immediately next to the down ramp. Allow your dog to get onto the table and from there have him step onto the ramp of the obstacle. When you first start teaching the contact obstacles, you will need the help of a training partner so there is a person on both sides of the dog to prevent him from slipping off the ramp.

Chapter 16

Climbing to the Highest Peak

Commands for the A-frame are usually "A-frame," "climb," or "scramble."

Goal: To Have Your Dog Stop at the Bottom of the A-frame

When you introduce the A-frame, set it at a low angle so that your dog can descend without sliding. In addition, place a cone at both corners of the bottom of the ramp. If the ramp is too steep, you will discover that the force of gravity may pull your dog's rear past his front as he comes down the ramp. Set the apex of the A-frame at about three feet. When the time comes to raise the A-frame, it can be raised an inch at a time.

Step 1

Double-leash your dog so that you and your partner can control him from both sides should he decide to jump off the ramp. Place him on the down ramp of the A-frame so that he is on your left, about one foot above the target. Tell him, "Look, get it," point to the food, and have him move down the ramp until he reaches the target. As he eats the food, tell him, "Wait," and place several pieces of food, one after the other, on the lid or ramp and allow him to eat them also. Do not allow him to move

154

away from the bottom of the contact. Praise him all the time you are putting down the food. Why not give him the food from your hand? You want him to focus on the contact. After he has remained in the spot you have chosen for about ten to fifteen seconds, give him his release word and allow him to leave the obstacle. Repeat this several times with him on your left. Then switch places with your partner and work the dog on your right.

Step 2

Once he has the idea of what is required, gradually place him higher up the ramp so that eventually he has to move several feet before he reaches the target. However, do not raise the height of the A-frame. You can dispense with the help of your training partner once you can see your dog does not need any assistance on the ramp.

Goal: To Teach Your Dog to Stay on the Contact, Without Command, Until Released

There are times in the obedience ring when the single command you give to your dog covers several behaviors in one exercise. A perfect example is retrieve-over-the-high-jump. You tell your dog to fetch and then expect him to leave your side, take the jump, pick up the dumbbell, return over the jump and sit in front, all with you issuing only one command. For some reason, people making the transition to agility feel they need to give their dogs a command for every single action. They would not consider doing this in obedience. Eventually you must put the responsibility on your dog to stop on the contacts, just as you expect him to take the jump in both directions in the retrieve-over-the-jump exercise in open. The sooner you expect him to stop on his own on the contacts, the better.

Step 1

Put your dog on the down ramp. Give him the command, "Look, get it," and send him down the ramp to the bottom and allow him to eat the food. Tell him, "Wait," and then start to walk away from the ramp while, at the same time, putting tension on the leash. From previous experience he should know what tension on the leash is all about. You should have used this technique when teaching him to stay on the pause table. If he stays on the contact, praise him, return to him, and then put a piece of food on the lid or ramp as a reward for staying. If your dog begins to leave the contact zone, verbally correct him by saying something like, "Hey, you are supposed to wait." If you can, physically pick him up and reposition him in the area where he is supposed to stop. Repeat the exercise until he resists your pull every time.

Step 2

Repeat the same exercise, but no longer tell him, "Wait" as you start to walk away from the ramp. If he stays, return to praise and treat him. If he leaves, correct him by replacing him on the contact.

Goal: To Have Your Dog Go over the A-frame

Once your dog is remaining on the contact without having to be reminded to wait as you walk away, then you can have him go up and over the A-frame. Place two cones at the bottom corners of the up ramp, just as you did at the bottom of the down ramp. You will need the assistance of your training partner once more. It is important that your dog have a straight-on approach to the ramp. If he approaches from the side, he may still be able to get onto the ramp. However, he may continue forward and slide off the other side. (See Figure 16-1.) With your

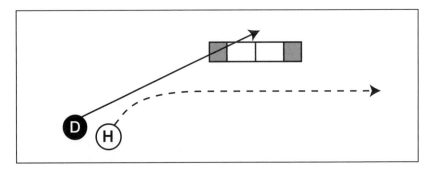

Figure 16-1. A dog may slip off the A-frame if he approaches it at an angle.

dog on leash and running between two people, you should be able to get him to run up the center of the ramp. You do not want your dog to stop at the apex of the A-frame. He should move over the obstacle in one single motion from start to finish.

Step 1

With your dog double-leashed, start with him about eight feet from the bottom of the up ramp. Say, "Climb," or whatever command you have chosen for the A-frame. Along with your partner, run with your dog toward the up ramp. With the A-frame set low, he should have no difficulty reaching the apex. As he goes over the top, say, "Look, get it," point at the food, and have him move to the bottom of the down ramp. Keep him on the contact for several seconds, then praise him, and give him his release word. Repeat this several times with him on both your left and right sides. If he has no problems going up and down the A-frame, you may dispense with the help of your training partner.

Step 2

Run with him and send him over the A-frame. Make sure the leash does not tighten. When he is in the contact area, continue forward to test him to see if he will remain on the contact.

Step 3

Remove the leash.

Step 4

Slowly increase the height of the A-frame. As the ramp becomes steeper, your dog's rear end may start to move sideways as he comes down the ramp. You may need the assistance of your training partner once more since you both may need to reach out with your hands to guide his rear to prevent him from sliding off the edge. With experience, he will learn to control his rear end so that he descends the ramp in a straight line. Ideally your dog should put his weight on his rear, rather than use his front end as a brake.

Goal: To Introduce an Obstacle Before and After the A-frame

Step 1

As your dog gains experience going over the A-frame, place a single bar jump about fifteen to eighteen feet in front of it. Because he is taking a jump first, he should ascend the up ramp with greater speed.

Step 2

Place a jump about fifteen to eighteen feet beyond the bottom of the down ramp. Seeing the jump as he descends from the apex may encourage your dog to leave the contact prematurely. After he has stopped on the contact, tell him, "Go jump" and then run with him toward the jump. He should leave the contact at speed. If he is slow, it may be because he is uncertain that it is permissible to leave to go to another obstacle. After all, you have spent several training sessions demanding he stay on the contact. Now you have changed the rules, and he may become confused temporarily.

Step 3

Replace the jumps with tunnels, the tire jump, spread jumps, and the table so that he encounters a variety of obstacles before and after the A-frame. Move to a schedule of random reinforcement on the contact. Remove the cones at the corners of the ramp.

Goal: To Introduce a Call-off

Although there may be an obstacle placed immediately ahead of your dog when he descends the ramp of the A-frame, it does not necessarily mean that obstacle is the next one on the course. It may be the next one on the course in the novice classes, but the obstacle could be a trap in the advanced classes.

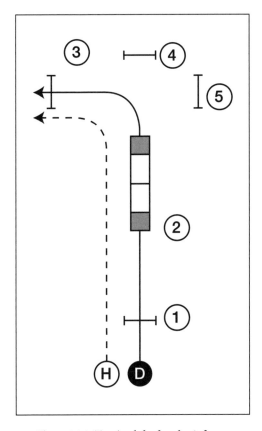

Figure 16-2. Turning left after the A-frame.

Place three obstacles beyond the down ramp of the A-frame. Place one straight ahead and the others at 90-degree angles, left and right, to the ramp. First, practice having your dog take the obstacle straight ahead of him. Then have him turn right or left to take an obstacle to the side. (See Figure 16-2.) Never allow your dog to leave the contact from the side. Always go straight ahead and then turn.

Goal: To Practice a "Cross in Front" and "Cross Behind" at the A-frame

The contact obstacles are a good place to switch sides on the course if you need to. Even if your dog is ahead of you, you should be able to catch up to him at a contact obstacle. As with switching sides on the jumps, a "cross in front" is safer than a "cross behind," but it is not always a smooth maneuver.

Step 1: "Cross in Front"

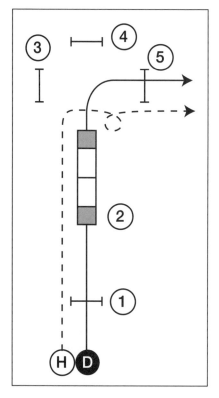

Figure 16-3. Crossing in front at the A-frame.

Place an obstacle before the A-frame and then three obstacles after it, as you did in the previous exercise. With your dog on your right, send him to the A-frame. While he is climbing the ramp, run past the A-frame, cross in front of the down ramp and pivot in toward the ramp so that your dog is now positioned on your left. Release him from the contact, turn right and send him over jump 5. (See Figure 16-3.) Repeat by running with your dog on your left, crossing in front of the down ramp, and then turning to the left and sending him over jump 3.

Step 2: "Cross Behind"

Set up the same exercise. With your dog on your right, run toward the A-frame but start to hold back as he approaches the up ramp, allowing him to get ahead

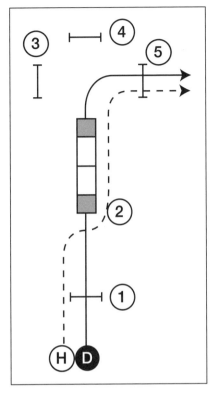

Figure 16-4 . Crossing behind
at the A-frame.

of you. As your dog moves up the ramp, cross behind it and then run past the A-frame with it on your left. (See Figure 16-4.) After your dog has paused on the contact, release him and have him turn right and take jump 5. When you do a "cross behind" on a contact obstacle, your dog may turn to see where you are going. You should get him used to the "cross behind" on the A-frame first, before trying it with the other contact obstacles. Because the A-frame is considerably wider, he is less likely to fall off it should he turn his head and body to see where you are going. Repeat by running with your dog on your left, crossing behind and passing the A-frame with it on your right, and then turning left and sending him over jump 3.

Do not always cross in front or behind at the A-frame. You do not want your dog to think that you will always be switching sides at this point on the course.

Goal: To Teach Your Dog to Square Up to Get on the A-frame

It is important that your dog approach a ramp straight on and not try to get on it from the side. Should he try to get on from the side he may simply continue sideways across the ramp and slide off the other side. (See Figure 16-1.)

Step 1

Stand with your dog on your left, perpendicular to the up ramp—about eight feet beyond the bottom of the ramp and five feet to the side of the A-frame. Tell him, "Get out, climb," then move forward and turn toward the ramp. (See Figure 16-5.) You may want to place cones or chicken wire sticking out from the bottom of the ramp so that your dog cannot cut the corner.

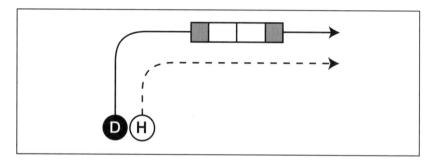

Figure 16-5. Teaching your dog to square up his approach to the A-frame.

Step 2

Stand off to the side with your back to the ramp. Tell your dog, "Get out, climb" as you step forward, and then turn 180 degrees to face the ramp. (See Figure 16-6.)

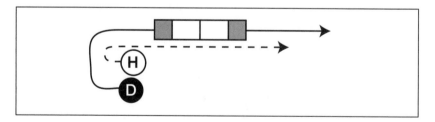

Figure 16-6. Teaching your dog to square up his approach to the A-frame.

With practice, your dog should automatically square up for a straight-on approach to the contact obstacles.

Chapter 17

Walking the Plank

The Dog Walk

Obstacle commands for the dog walk are usually "dog walk," "walk," or "plank."

You can introduce your dog to the dog walk once he has no difficulty negotiating the A-frame. In competition, the ramps of the dog walk are not as steep as those of the A-frame, but the board is only nine to twelve inches wide. This does not give a large dog much of a footing, and it is easy for any dog to fall off the dog walk if he is not paying attention to where he is going. I know of at least one dog that broke a leg when falling from the dog walk.

Some dog walks are adjustable in height, so if you can train on a low dog walk you should take advantage of that, until your dog has more experience with staying on the narrow board. If he should fall off, it will not be so far to the ground, and he is less likely to be injured. Another thing to take into consideration is the width of the dog walk. It is safer to train your dog on a twelve-inch-wide AKC dog walk than a nine-inch USDAA one. The three-inch difference in width between the two dog walks means your dog will find the AKC one 25 percent wider, and for him, that is a substantial difference. Most dogs, once they have become accustomed to negotiating a twelve-inch dog walk, do not seem to notice when faced with a narrower board. If your dog falls off a dog walk early on in training, he may never regain his confidence on that obstacle. Some dogs are more sure-footed than others and will never be afraid crossing a narrow board.

If you do not own contact equipment, a solution for getting your dog used to walking the plank is to purchase a board that is about 2″ × 12″ × 10′ to 2″ × 12″ × 12′ in size at a lumberyard. You can place the board on concrete blocks and accustom your dog to walking on top

Figure 17-1. Using cones next to the down ramp of the dog walk to give a dog a sense of security.

of a narrow board suspended just above the ground. You can lean the board up against the pause table and teach your dog to walk up and down it while it is on an angle. You can also place it on a piece of PVC pipe to simulate the movement of the seesaw.

Whether or not you have access to a regulation dog walk, you still must teach your dog to stop at the bottom of the plank, just as you taught him to stop at the bottom of the A-frame. You will find his rear is more likely to slip off the narrow plank of the dog walk than the wider ramp of the A-frame. Be sure to use your cones as a guide at the end of the board. (See Figure 17-1.) You will need the assistance of your training partner in the beginning, if only to help prevent your dog's rear from moving sideways as he comes down the ramp.

Goal: To Have Your Dog Stop at the Bottom of the Dog Walk

Because the plank is so narrow, it might be easier and safer to have your dog step onto the down ramp from the pause table, rather than trying to place him on the narrow plank. You will probably want your dog to stop on the dog walk contact in the same manner as you did on the A-frame. This would be either stopping with his two rear feet on the plank and his two front feet on the ground or stopping with all four feet on the plank. (See Figures 17-2A and 17-2B.) Position the treat in the same way as you did for the A-frame.

Step 1

Place your dog on the plank, near the bottom. With your partner on the left side and your dog double-leashed between you, tell him, "Look, get it." Have him move a few inches down the plank to reach the target. Tell him, "Wait," and while you keep him from leaving the contact, place several pieces of food, one after the other, on the margarine lid or the plank. Finally, give him his release word and then allow him to leave the contact. After several repetitions start over with him on your right.

Figure 17-2A. A dog stopping on the contact with two front feet on the ground and two rear feet on the board.

Figure 17-2B. A dog stopping on the contact by remaining on the end of the board.

Step 2

Once your dog is able to remain on the contact without falling off the narrow board, place him farther up the plank so he has to move several feet to reach the target. As long as he is not falling off the board, you may dispense with the help of your training partner. Have your dog move down the plank on both your left and your right.

Step 3

Test your dog by putting tension on the leash at the bottom of the plank, as you did with the A-frame.

Goal: To Have Your Dog Run Across the Dog Walk

You will need the assistance of your training partner once more. Double-leash your dog so that should he start to slip, you or your partner can catch him or break his fall. Place a cone at each corner of the up ramp.

Step 1

Remember to have your dog approach the up ramp straight on. Start with your dog about eight feet away from the bottom of the ramp, holding his leash in your right hand. When you give him the command for the dog walk, you should give a signal toward the obstacle with your left arm. As your dog begins to move along the plank, extend your left arm sideways so that you could touch him in the event that he starts to slip. Your partner should do the same on her side of the plank. (See Figure 17-3.) Give your dog the command you plan to use for the dog walk. Then with your partner, run toward the up ramp. The moment your dog crosses the middle section of the plank and starts his descent, tell him, "Look, get it" and then have him stop in the contact area and eat the treat. After several repetitions switch sides with your partner. Once your dog is crossing the dog walk with confidence, remove the leash. Continue to use a training partner in case your dog takes a misstep and starts to fall. Until he is more experienced at staying on the narrow board, it is a good idea always to have a spotter on both sides of the dog walk. Occasionally you will place several pieces of food, one after the other, on the plank or lid as an extra incentive for your dog to remain on the contact until released.

Figure 17-3. A dog moving down the ramp on leash, between his handler and her training partner. Notice the placement of their hands, which are extended to prevent the dog from slipping off the board.

Step 2

Add a jump before and after the dog walk, as you did with the A-frame.

Step 3

Replace the jumps with other agility obstacles, but do not include the A-frame immediately before or after the dog walk. It is most unlikely that there will be two contact obstacles in a row. Remove the cones and move to a schedule of random reinforcement on the contacts. Always carry treats in your pocket to reward a fast execution of the dog walk or a solid wait on the contact. If you are training on a low dog walk, raise it to competition height.

A problem may arise once your dog becomes confident at getting on the narrow plank. He may fail to touch the up contact as he mounts the ramp, and this is cause for elimination at a trial. Missing the up contact is more likely to occur when a dog has a long stride or moves very fast. Your dog may already be missing the up contact on the A-frame. However, AKC rules do not require a dog to touch the up contact on the

A-frame—only on the dog walk and seesaw. There are several solutions to prevent him from missing the up contact on these obstacles. You might try giving the command "easy" as you approach the ramp. Many dogs recognize that command from obedience, particularly those that tend to forge on heeling! However, if your dog comes to a complete stop at the base of the dog walk, you may receive a penalty for a refusal. When I have encountered missed up contacts in the past, I have found the best solution is to place some food partway up the up ramp. When placed in this way, my dog can only reach the food once he has all four of his feet on the plank. If you place the target close to the beginning of the ramp, your dog may stop to check the ramp before he gets on it, incurring a refusal. Another solution may be to place a "hoop" at the start of the dog walk so that your dog has to pass under it to get onto the ramp. You can also lay several jump bars spaced several feet apart on the ground leading to the up ramp. This forces a dog to change the length of his stride on his approach to the obstacle. However, once these bars are no longer in place, many dogs go back to their regular stride and then leap high onto the ramp once more.

Step 4

Introduce a turn coming off the dog walk, as you did with the A-frame. Do not forget to have your dog leave the contact and then make the turn.

Step 5

When you introduce a change in sides, take great care if you practice a "cross behind." Should your dog look back to see where you went, he just might step off the dog walk out into space. It would probably be smart to use only a "cross in front" until your dog has a lot more experience on the dog walk.

The Seesaw

Obstacle commands for the seesaw are usually "seesaw," "teeter," or "tip it."

You should leave the teaching of the seesaw until your dog has been moving confidently across the dog walk for several weeks. Some dogs become afraid when the seesaw starts to move, so do not be in a rush to introduce it. One false step and you may have a dog that will never get on a seesaw again.

Some trainers change how they want their dogs to stop on the seesaw contact. If they have their dogs stop on the A-frame and dog walk with two feet on and two feet off, they may require their dogs to stop with all four feet on the ramp of the seesaw. (See Figure 17-2B.) This is a question of personal preference. It will probably be less confusing to your dog if you require identical contact performance for all contact obstacles.

If you are going to have your dog assume the two feet on, two feet off position on the contact, then you need to tip the board to see where to place the margarine tub lid. You should place it as far from the end of the seesaw plank as you did with the dog walk.

If you bought that ten- to twelve-foot plank I recommended, you can get your dog used to the movement of the board when he is close to the ground. Take a short section of one-inch PVC pipe and place it under the board, midway from each end. Then put your margarine tub lid beyond the end of the board, or place a piece of sticky food on the far end of the plank. You should use something that will not fall off when the board hits the ground. Colby cheese or liver sausage works well. When introducing your dog to the seesaw, I have found it is better to put food on the end of the plank to give your dog something on which to focus. You can always move the food to the ground once your dog becomes accustomed to the movement of the plank.

With your dog on leash, have him walk along the plank. Then as he reaches the midpoint, grasp his collar to give him added stability and continue walking. Encourage him to continue moving as the board tips. Tell him, "Look, get it" just as he passes the midpoint. With luck, he will never notice the movement of the board because his mind will be focused on the food at the end. Ideally, once he gains confidence your dog will not slow up as the board begins to tip, even when you are no longer holding his collar. The exception to this will be with the smaller breeds. These dogs often have to ride the board down to the ground rather than keep on moving. The less the dog weighs, the farther he will have to travel along the board before it begins to tip. (See Figure 17-4.) A small, light dog will almost reach the end of the board before his weight will make it tip, so he may need to stop and then ride the seesaw to the ground. Should the dog continue moving, he could reach the end while the board is still up in the air. Leaving the seesaw before the board touches the ground is known as a "fly-off" and is cause for elimination.

Figure 17-4. A small dog stopping and riding the seesaw board to the ground.

When your dog is paying little attention to the movement of the board, substitute a larger-diameter PVC pipe so that the board has farther to tip. You can often find discarded PVC or sewer pipe at building sites. Alternatively, you can get a six-inch-diameter heavy-duty cardboard end roll, found where they print newspapers. You need something round to place under the board to simulate the action of a seesaw.

Formal Seesaw Training

The seesaw is constructed so that when it is not in use, the up ramp always remains on the ground, while the down ramp stays up in the air. When you begin formal seesaw training, place your dog on the up ramp, facing down. You will need to teach him to descend the ramp, as you did with the dog walk.

Because you have already introduced him to the dog walk, introducing him to the stationary seesaw should be easy. Gradually place him farther up the ramp until he is moving to the end of the board from the middle of the seesaw.

Goal: To Teach Your Dog to Tip the Seesaw

I have found two ways to teach this exercise successfully. One involves starting your dog from the table and, from there, having him step onto the seesaw. The other uses the help of a spotter who controls the tip of the board while you control the dog. The spotter is your training partner.

1. Teaching the Seesaw from the Table

First, tip the board. Then place a cone just off to each side where the end of the down ramp will make contact with the ground. If possible, make the table height twenty-four inches; then put the table under the end of the up ramp. The seesaw board will be pointing slightly toward the ground. When your dog tips the board, it will not drop nearly as far as it would if the end of the up ramp were touching the ground.

Step 1

Place your margarine tub lid beyond where the end of the ramp touches the ground or place some sticky food on the end of the board. If you do not want to contaminate the end of the seesaw, place the food on a margarine tub lid, which you can then anchor to the end of the board with large rubber bands. Have your dog get on the table. With your dog on leash on your left and your training partner on the opposite side of the board, say, "Teeter," or whatever command you have chosen to use for the seesaw. Grasp your dog by his collar and guide him onto the board. He is already used to going across the plank of the dog walk, so he should willingly make his way onto the seesaw. Be sure he has a straight-on approach. Moreover, watch to see that his back legs do not slip from the table as he leaves the table and steps onto the narrower board. Dogs have been known to step onto the board with their front legs and then forget about their rear legs and fall to the ground. As your dog reaches the halfway point say, "Look, get it" and then reach forward with your right hand and grasp the edge of the board. As your dog's weight starts tipping the board, slow its fall. Your partner should be doing the same thing on the other side. Make your dog remain in the contact area until you release him. Repeat a number of times and then switch with your partner so that your dog is on your right.

Step 2

If possible, lower the table to twenty inches so that the seesaw board is parallel to the ground. When the board tips, it will have slightly farther to fall. After several successful repetitions with you on both sides of the seesaw, lower the table to sixteen inches. Your dog will now have to ascend the ramp slightly before his weight causes the board to tip. Finally, set the table to twelve inches. If your dog is still successfully negotiating the seesaw, eliminate using the table.

Step 3

When you no longer need to start your dog from the table, place a cone at each corner of the up ramp to guide him onto the board. After several repetitions with your dog on both sides, remove the leash. Incorporate a hand signal for the obstacle, as you did with the dog walk.

Step 4

Move to Step 4 of the next section.

2. Teaching the Seesaw by Using a Spotter

The job of your spotter is to control the tip of the board. In the beginning, your dog will be on leash on your left, and your spotter should stand to the left of the seesaw, midway between the middle and end of the board. Your job will be to control your dog should he try to jump off the seesaw as it starts to tip. Place two cones and the food at the end of the ramp, as suggested in the previous section, and a cone on each side of the up ramp. (See Figure 15-2 in Chapter 15.)

Step 1

Give your seesaw command and approach the obstacle from about eight feet away, as you did with the dog walk. As your dog starts to move up the board, tell him, "Look, get it" and point toward the end of the board. As your dog's weight begins to tip the board, your spotter should control its descent to the ground. Encourage your dog to keep moving while the board is slowly tipping. Make sure your dog remains on the contact until you release him. After several repetitions have your spotter move to the right of the seesaw, and have your dog run on your right. Occasionally, place several pieces of food, one at a time, on the end of the ramp or the margarine tub lid on the ground and make your dog stay on the contact for ten to fifteen seconds, or more.

Step 2

Practice off leash, sending your dog ahead of you to the seesaw. Your spotter will continue to control the speed at which the board tips.

Step 3

Keep your spotter in position, but allow your dog to tip the board. Your spotter can always control the board if your dog is moving too fast or catch your dog if he starts to fall off the plank.

Step 4

Make sure your dog remains on the contact when you apply tension to the leash or pull forward on his collar.

Step 5

Add a jump before and after the seesaw. Remember that your dog will be getting on the seesaw at greater speed when he takes a jump first. This may affect the speed at which he crosses over the board. Add different obstacles before and after the seesaw. Remove the cones. Place him on a schedule of random reinforcement on the contacts. Always carry treats in your pocket to reward a fast execution of the seesaw or a solid wait on the contact.

Step 6

Practice turning your dog to the right and left when he leaves the seesaw.

Step 7

Introduce a "cross in front" at the seesaw. Hold off practicing a "cross behind" for several weeks. Should your dog look back to see where you are going, he may fall off the seesaw. You do not want him to have a bad experience at this point in his training.

If your dog starts missing the up contact of the seesaw, refer to the section on the dog walk for suggestions about how to correct this.

No matter how carefully you introduce the seesaw, some dogs are afraid of getting on the board once they realize it is going to move. I have found that placing treats every few inches all the way along the board can help them overcome their fear. Unfortunately, this method will encourage your dog to move slowly, but once he loses his fear of the seesaw, his speed should increase. Sometimes you have to sacrifice speed to get your dog to perform the exercise. As your dog reaches the point at which the board will start to tip, slowly start to lower it to the ground. Because your dog can see another treat immediately in front of him, rather than at the far end of the board, he should worry less about the movement because he will be focused on the treat. It may take some practice to find the exact spot you need to place one of the treats so that your dog reaches it just as the board starts to tip. There is nothing wrong with having your dog stop as the board starts to move. It will only cost you a few seconds of time. It is better to have your dog stop and remain on the board until it touches the ground than to have him refuse to get on the seesaw.

The Crossover

The crossover is in the shape of a plus sign. It looks rather like two dog walks meeting at right angles. However, instead of there being a long plank between the up and down ramps, the crossover has a platform in the middle where all four ramps meet. You seldom see a crossover used on a course, probably because they take up so much space and space is at a premium at many facilities. Since I have been involved in agility, I have only once run into a crossover at a trial. I was not certain how my dogs would handle it, but it did not present them with a problem. Most dogs ascending the crossover ramp are unlikely to look right or left as they cross the platform in the middle and go down the opposite side. They think they are on an unusual-looking dog walk. Should you need to turn your dog right or left at the middle, a well-timed "wait" command as the dog reaches the platform should be adequate to stop him. Then you can turn him in the correct direction.

Chapter 18

Contact Consternation

Most A-frames in use at trials are similar to each other in construction and appearance. However, some dog walks are bouncy, while others hardly move as the dog runs across their span. Some seesaws have slats on the plank, and others do not, and seesaws tip differently from each other. Dogs notice these details, and this can affect their performance. The more experience your dog has negotiating different contact obstacles, the better he will perform in a trial.

NADAC regulations do not require slats on the dog walk, while AKC rules require the ramps to have slats. When running my experienced dog at a NADAC trial, she suddenly stopped halfway up the ramp of the dog walk. She remained frozen for several seconds before gingerly continuing her ascent. Once she reached the cross ramp, she completed the obstacle perfectly. I could not figure out what had caused her to stop until it dawned on me that without slats on the ramp my dog believed she was on the seesaw. When the board did not start to tip as she reached the halfway point, she became worried and came to a stop.

AKC does not require slats on the seesaw, and my own seesaw does not have any. However, many seesaws used in competition do have slats. The only time my dogs have ever had a fly-off is when a seesaw with slats was used on the course. Because I did not pay attention and tell my dogs, "Easy," they thought they were on the dog walk and raced to the end of the board. This resulted in a fly-off.

Many green dogs incur refusals at the contact obstacles. This sometimes happens because the dog notices that the obstacle appears to be different than the one he is used to using. Sometimes a dog gets on a contact obstacle, feels the difference, and immediately jumps off. Then he may refuse to get on the next one because he has lost his confidence.

Much of the time it is the handler who causes the dog to refuse to get on the contact obstacle. Handlers run right at the obstacle and then at the last moment veer off to the side, taking the dog with them. Others run right at the obstacle, which causes them to push their dogs away from the ramp.

Some handlers approach the obstacle at an angle, which allows the dog to get on and then continue over the side. It is better to take an extra second or two to line your dog up for a straight-on approach. Handlers sometimes encourage their dogs to speed up as they come down the ramp, and the dog jumps off instead.

Take any opportunity presented to introduce your dog to different contact obstacles in training. If you have entered a novice agility class and the trial-giving club allows obstacle familiarization, take advantage of it.

Chapter 19

The Ins and Outs of Agility

Commands for the weave poles are usually "weave," "poles," or "wiggle." If you were to ask a spectator at an agility trial what obstacle he found the most impressive, you would likely be told, "The weave poles." There is no question about it. A dog racing through the weave poles is a spectacular sight to see. If you take a moment to think about it, dogs that perform well on the weave poles have two things in common. They have rhythm and focus.

If you get an opportunity to go to an agility competition before you begin teaching weave poles, take time to watch dogs going through the poles. It will be a learning experience. You may discover a number of dogs weaving in a similar manner, and it will be obvious that these exhibitors probably train together. Take time to talk to these exhibitors and try to learn their weave pole secret. You may want to use their method to teach your own dog. Dogs that belong to members of Flash Paws Agility Club in Houston, Texas, all appear to have great style going through the weave poles. The club director, Jane Simmons-Moake, told me that the school trains using offset poles on a regular basis. In addition, the pole holders are made using large springs so that the poles move out of the way as the dog races through them. She kindly gave me the design for this base, and I made my dogs a Christmas present. This base cost more to make than one I had purchased, but it improved my dogs' weave pole performance by several seconds. A couple of seconds does not sound like a lot, but it can mean the difference between qualifying with a clean run, getting time faults, or not making time at all.

A dog that has rhythm going through the weave poles places his feet exactly the same way all the way through the poles. Some dogs hop their front feet from side to side across the centerline as they go through the poles, while others place their feet right or left of the centerline. Both ways are correct. This has become known as the weave pole dance. (See Figures 19-1A, 19-1B, and 19-1C.) Although weave poles are supposed to flex, the design of many bases causes the poles to remain rigid. Many dogs dislike bumping into rigid poles, and this may be one reason a dog may slow down when entering or running through the poles. Flash Paws has come up with a design for flexible poles, which bend easily as the dog runs through them. (See Figure 19-2.) Flexible poles allow the dog to remain close to the centerline, saving vital seconds. You will find directions for making this type of pole in Appendix B.

If you were to ask ten successful obedience trainers how they teach the "go outs," you would probably get ten different answers. If you asked

*Figure 19-1A. Small dog hopping back and forth through
the weave poles on her front legs.*

Figure 19-1B. A medium-sized dog stepping on both sides of the centerline of the weave pole base.

Figure 19-1C. A large dog stepping on both sides of the centerline of the weave pole base. Notice that all three dogs in Figures 19-1A, 19-1B, and 19-1C are focused on the poles ahead.

Figure 19-2. A flexible weave pole.

ten successful agility competitors how they teach weave poles, you would likely get ten different responses. Trainers in different areas of the country favor different methods of teaching the poles. Since I have used chicken-wire chutes as guides in obedience, I favor the guide wires with offset poles method. In the beginning, the offset poles can be set wide enough to form a channel for the dog to run through, and the guide wires keep the dog from leaving the channel. (See Figure 19-3.) The line of poles is gradually moved together. Many trainers prefer to use slanted poles, which start out looking like a line of V's and are slowly raised to the upright position. There is also the straight line of poles with guides method. (See Figure 19-4.) Some trainers use their hand to guide their dogs through the poles. As with "go outs," there is no "right" way to teach weave poles. Use whatever you feel comfortable using or what your instructor recommends.

Figure 19-3. Offset weave poles making a channel for the dog.
Guide wires prevent the dog from leaving the channel.

Figure 19-4. A straight line of weave poles with guides.

I equate weave pole training with "go out" training in utility. You have probably discovered that "go outs" often take a year or more to perfect, and during that time you need to practice them on a regular basis. Weave poles take just as long to perfect, and you should practice them daily. For this reason, the weave poles is one of the pieces of equipment that is essential to own. Because dogs are context-oriented, once your dog begins to understand the exercise, you need to set up your weave poles in many different locations. From experience, dogs learning to do the poles do not always recognize them if you move the poles some-where new. This is a similar issue to a dog not recognizing where to go on the "sendaway" when you move the location of your obedience ring. You can certainly make your own weave poles, but because you need to take them to different locations, it might be better to purchase bases that hinge in the middle. This way you can fold them and transport them easily in your vehicle.

In AKC competition there are no weave poles in the novice standard class, and only six poles allowed in the jumpers class. At the advanced level, there can be as few as six weave poles and as many as twelve. Most of the time, courses use an even number of poles, but occasionally they use a set of odd-numbered poles. This can present a problem if your dog is not used to exiting the poles from both sides. At the novice level in NADAC competition, you might have only five weave poles on a course. Owning a set of poles that you can switch between odd and even numbers is something worth considering. At least one weave pole manufacturer has addressed this problem. You can easily remove both end-pole supports on each six-pole hinged base. This way, you can practice using only four, five, or six poles when you use one base, and when you add a second base, you can use a set of nine, ten, eleven, or twelve poles.

Because it takes so long to perfect the weave poles, the training of this exercise should start the moment you become involved in agility. Some trainers believe in teaching their dogs to weave through all twelve poles right from the start, while others believe in starting with four poles and slowly adding to that number. A dog learning to weave through only four poles may be more successful in the beginning. However, I do not think a dog learns rhythm when he starts out with only four poles. Weave pole training is physically tiring for your dog, and this is one reason it takes so long to perfect this exercise. Your dog is using muscles he is not used to using and may tire quickly. Therefore, the number of times you can have him run through the poles may be limited.

There is a right and wrong way for the dog to enter the weave poles. He must enter the poles with the first pole on his left. Entering the poles incorrectly incurs a refusal. If your dog skips a pole during the sequence, that is also counted as a refusal. When a dog races through the poles, it is sometimes difficult to know whether he missed one. However, there is a rule that will indicate whether he completed the poles successfully, based on whether the poles are odd or even numbered. This is known as the ROLE rule. If there is an odd number of poles, your dog will exit the poles to the right. If there is an even number, he will exit to the left. Right Odd, Left Even—ROLE. If you are using guide wires, you should always use an even number of poles because, otherwise, your dog will only be able to enter the poles correctly from one direction. You will be unable to send your dog through the poles, turn him around, and then send him back the other way.

If you use the offset or slanted pole method, in the beginning your dog will be running through a channel, which he will find less tiring than weaving back and forth. For this reason, you may be able to do more repetitions than you might if the poles were set in a straight line.

Teaching Weave Poles Using the Offset or Slanted Poles Method

Goal: To Teach Your Dog to Run Through a Line of Poles

If you use the offset pole method, in the beginning set the poles far enough apart so that your dog can easily run down the center of the poles. In addition, use the guide wires if you have them. Position the wires on the poles so that they are just below your dog's shoulder. (See Figure 19-5.) At close to shoulder height, it will be difficult for him to step over or duck under the guides. If you do not have any guides, you can set a temporary fence of baby gates on both sides of the offset poles to prevent your dog from leaving the line. You can do the same thing to keep him from leaving the line of slanted poles.

Whenever my dogs have come out of the poles during training or competition, it is usually because they have turned their heads to look

Figure 19-5. Guides set at just below the dog's shoulder.

at me or at another obstacle on the course. When they have successfully completed running through the poles, they have been looking straight ahead.

Step 1

Sit your dog immediately in front of the entrance to the weave poles. Tell him to "wait/stay," and then walk to the other end. Hold a motivator in front of you and tell him, "Come, weave" or use whatever command you plan to use for this obstacle. Most dogs trained in obedience will come straight down the channel. If your dog refuses to move, or tries to go around, then you may need to put the leash on and walk him between the line of poles several times. This should make him familiar with this new concept. Repeat calling him through the poles several times until he consistently runs through the channel with confidence.

Step 2

Put your dog on a "sit stay" immediately in front of and to the right of the first pole, and then place his motivator several feet beyond the last pole. Place the motivator up on something so your dog will run with his head up. Because it is easy to cheat on the weave poles, if you use food you may want to use a food tube instead. Stand with your dog on your left. Tell him, "Look, go weave" and then run with him down the line of poles toward the target. As he passes the final pole tell him, "Get it." If you are using a food tube, you will have to take the treat from the tube and reward him by hand. Repeat several times and then switch to having him run down the poles when he is on your right. Remember that many courses are set up so that there is a weave-on-right advantage. Therefore, practice many more repetitions of the weave poles with your dog on your right than on your left.

Step 3

Position your dog a foot from the entrance to the weave poles so that he has to move forward to reach the first pole. Gradually move him farther back until he properly enters the poles from several feet away.

Step 4

Move the line of offset poles a little closer together, or decrease the angle of the slanted poles by a few inches. Continue to run with your dog down the line of poles as you slowly reduce the distance the poles are offset from each other or reduce the angle of the slanted poles. Soon your dog will be starting to bend his body.

Step 5

Gradually move the offset poles together until they are only two inches apart, or set the slanted poles almost perpendicular to the ground. You should probably keep your dog at this stage of training for several weeks. If you are using guide wires, rather than removing them completely begin to raise them up the poles. First, raise the wires in the middle while leaving the guides at shoulder height on the first and last two poles. This is similar to loosening the tie-downs when teaching scent articles in utility. You do not want your dog to miss the entry or exit. If your dog begins to miss poles when the wires are not there to guide him, all you have to do is slide the wires back down the poles.

Step 6

Raise the guide wires up on the first and last poles to see if your dog continues to enter the poles correctly. Remove the target and go to a schedule of random reinforcement. Always carry a motivator on you so that you can reinforce an exceptionally fast performance.

If at any time your dog starts making mistakes on the poles, immediately slide the guides back down for several training sessions. I have found that once you remove the tie-downs on articles in utility, you probably have to put them back on the articles several times before your dog is ready to show. The same holds true for using guides on the weave poles. Just because your dog can do the weave poles correctly one day does not mean you will not have to return to using guides again. When you move your scent articles to a new location, you will probably have to tie them down again. When you move your weave poles to a new location, you should put the guides back on. If you are training with slanted poles, you may have to increase the angle of the slant if your dog has problems with the poles in a different location.

Step 7

Teach your dog to find the entrance to the weave poles. Many dogs miss the entry to the poles because they are approaching them at an angle. You can use a similar approach to the way you taught your dog to find the entrance to the tunnel. Be sure to use guides for this in the beginning so that your dog enters correctly, no matter the angle of his approach. (See Figures 19-6A and 19-6B.) If you are using slanted poles, return to having them at a slight angle when you work on your dog finding the entrance. The steeper the angle your dog approaches the poles, the tighter he will have to turn to get in. If he approaches from the right, he will have to turn tight around pole 2. If he approaches from the left, he will have to turn tight around pole 1. (See Figures 19-7A and 19-7B.)

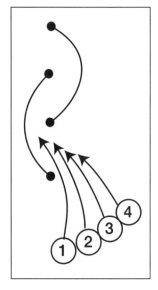

Figure 19-6A. Teaching the dog to find the weave pole entrance from the right.

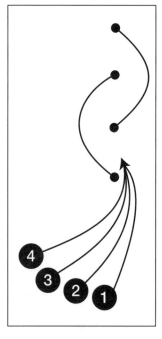

Figure 19-6B. Teaching the dog to find the weave pole entrance from the left.

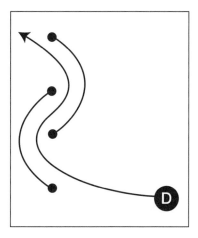

Figure 19-7A. Dog having to make a sharp turn around pole 2.

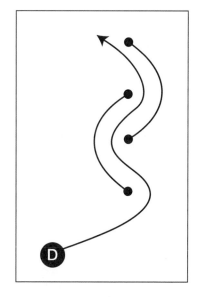

Figure 19-7B. Dog having to make a sharp turn around pole 1.

Step 8

Set the poles in a straight line and remove the guides completely.

Teaching Weave Poles Using Straight Poles and Guides

If you do not have guide wires to place on the poles, you can still channel your dog correctly into the weaves. To guide your dog down the line of poles, you can use two exercise pens, baby gates with feet, or some temporary fencing to take the place of the guide wires. It would be best to begin by using only four poles, or six at the most. Because your poles are in a straight line, your dog will have to bend his body right from the start, and this will be tiring.

Set up a line of four or six poles. If you are using only four poles without wire guides, place one ex-pen to the left of the line so that the first two panels of the ex-pen form a V, beginning with pole 1 and ending at pole 3. If you are using baby gate sections, place one edge against the first pole and position the other edge against the second baby gate to form a V. You will need two sections of baby gates for each side when using four poles. Place the second ex-pen to the right, with the edges of the two panels touching poles 2 and 4. Use a similar setup with two

Figure 19-8A. Use of ex-pens and baby gates with feet as guides.

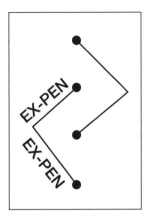

Figure 19-8B. How to set up baby gate or ex-pen guides when using 4 poles.

more baby gates. (See Figures 19-8A and 19-8B.) If you are using six poles, then make the ex-pens or baby gates into a W. With the ex-pen on the left, have the edge of the panels touch poles 1-3-5, and the edge of the panels on the right touch poles 2-4-6. (See Figure 19-8C.) By setting the pens or baby gates up in this way, you will have a zigzag channel for your dog to move through. If you are using temporary fencing, place the support stakes to the left or right of the poles and make the fence into a semicircle. (See Figure 19-8D.)

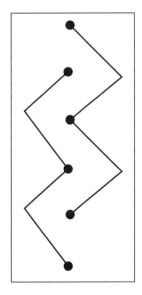

Figure 19-8C. How to set up baby gate or ex-pen guides when using 6 poles.

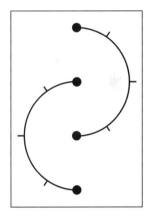

Figure 19-8D. How to set up guides using temporary fencing.

Goal: To Teach Your Dog to Weave Through Four or Six Poles

Step 1

Place a motivator out beyond the last pole as suggested in Step 2 of the previous section. With your dog on your left, tell him, "Look, go weave," and as he passes the last pole, say, "Get it." Repeat this several times and then have him go through the poles when he is on your right. Gradually move him farther back from the entrance to the poles.

Figure 19-9. Slowly move the guides away from the poles.

Step 2

After many repetitions, slowly pull the ex-pens or temporary fencing away from the poles so that your dog has the choice of going around the correct pole or missing it. (See Figure 19-9.) If he tries to skip going around the poles as you pull the fence away, put him on leash and guide him around the poles. After several repetitions remove the leash, and then try again. Do not forget, teaching the weave poles takes months of practice.

Step 3

If you are only using four poles, once he is successfully going around the four poles, add two more. Do not exceed six poles until your dog is consistently going around all six. Move to a schedule of random reinforcement.

Step 4

Teach your dog to find the entrance to the weave poles. Many dogs miss the entry to the poles because they are approaching them at an angle. You can use an approach similar to the way you taught your dog to find the entrance to the tunnel. (See Figures 19-6A and 19-6B.) Be sure to use guides for this in the beginning so that your dog enters correctly, no matter the angle of his approach. The steeper the angle your dog approaches the poles, the tighter he will have to turn to get in. If he approaches from the right, he will have to turn tight around pole 2. If he approaches from the left, he will have to turn tight around pole 1. (See Figures 19-10A and 19-10B.)

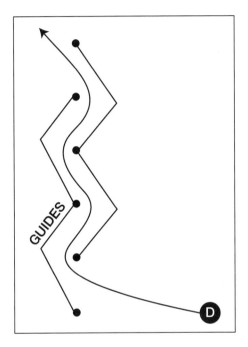

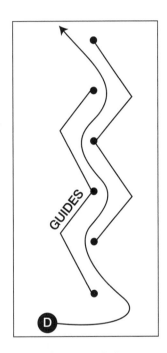

Figure 19-10A. Dog approaching poles from the right and having to make a sharp turn around pole 2.

Figure 19-10B. Dog approaching poles from the left and having to make a sharp turn around pole 1.

Finally, remove the guides, but be prepared to replace them if necessary.

If you find you need to put your dog back on leash periodically, you might consider investing in some shorter poles to use just for this purpose. It is awkward to guide a dog around standard height poles since they tend to catch on the leash. However, it is easy to guide your dog with poles that are about twenty-four to twenty-seven inches high.

Since PVC pipe is cheap to buy and easy to cut, it may well be worth owning some short poles.

Goal: To Add Obstacles Before and After the Weave Poles

No matter which method you select to teach the weave poles, eventually you will need to include the weave poles in your sequence of obstacles. As with all the other obstacles, your dog's speed approaching the weave poles is likely to be faster following a jump, a tunnel, or other obstacles.

Step 1

If you need to, reset the guides. Place a jump about twenty feet in front of the weave poles and your motivator a few feet beyond the last pole. Send your dog over the jump and into the weave poles. Practice with him on both your right and your left.

Step 2

Add an obstacle after the weave poles. A dog will often miss the last one or two poles because he is thinking about the next obstacle in the sequence. He forgets to concentrate on the job at hand, which is to weave through the entire line of poles. I like to use a panel jump or tunnel after the weave poles because this type of obstacle easily blocks the dog's view of the motivator. I use a target for a longer time than I do with the other obstacles because I want my dog to continue looking ahead. (See Figure 19-11.)

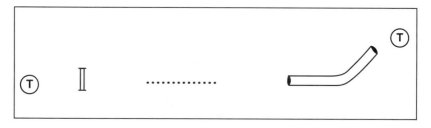

Figure 19-11. Target can be hidden by panel jump or tunnel.

Step 3

Have your dog turn right or left after he leaves the poles. Do not start to turn your body until your dog has passed the last pole (See Figure 19-12A.). If you do, he is likely to turn with you and miss the exit. (See Figure 19-12B.)

Step 4

A "cross in front" is difficult to do on the weave poles unless you are faster than your dog. Many dogs come out of the poles if their handler gets out in front of them. However, you should still practice this type of side switch on the weave poles, although you may never use it in competition. It is easier to do a "cross behind," and this is something you should practice routinely. Many courses are designed to have a switch of sides at the poles.

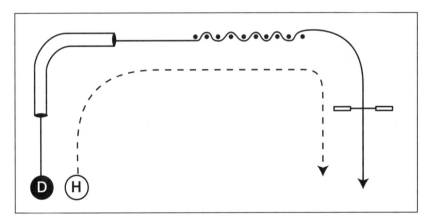

Figure 19-12A. Handler turns toward the next obstacle after the dog has completed going through the poles.

Weave Woes

There are three major errors made by dogs on the weave poles: (1) incorrect entry, (2) missing a pole during the sequence, and (3) coming out of the poles prematurely. These problems are often handler-induced.

If a dog misses a weave pole entry, particularly when there is a straight-on approach, look at where the handler is in relation to the poles. The handler will often be beyond the first pole when the dog reaches the weaves, and the dog may enter at the second or third pole instead. A rule of thumb for a handler is to not pass the line of the first weave pole until the dog has entered. Dogs that are the most successful on the poles are the ones that enter ahead of the handler.

I have had my dogs miss the last pole when odd-numbered poles were used at a trial. Now that I own poles that can be adapted to odd and even numbers, that is no longer a concern. Missing a pole in the middle of the line often happens when a dog is moving at a high rate of speed, rather than because of handler error. The dog is simply moving too fast. However, dogs tend to come out of the poles if the handler begins to drift away from the line of poles, possibly in anticipation of moving

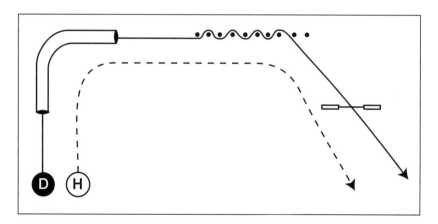

Figure 19-12B. Handler turns toward the next obstacle too soon,
pulling the dog out of the weave poles early.

toward the next obstacle in the sequence. When a dog misses a pole or two at the end, this is usually the fault of the handler. The handler knows where to go next and begins to make the turn before the dog gets through the line of poles. The dog notices the change in direction of the handler and comes out of the poles prematurely. (See Figure 19-12B.)

If the weave poles follow a tunnel, particularly the collapsed tunnel, a dog may not focus on the next obstacle until he is close to the weave pole entry. By then, it may be too late to enter correctly. Depending on the background and where the poles are located on the course, they may be difficult to see, and a dog may miss seeing them. At one trial I attended, the base of the poles was covered in dirt to make the poles more stable. A number of experienced dogs, including my own, missed the entry or failed to complete the poles. Since none of us had practiced without a visible base, the only conclusion we could draw was that our dogs did not recognize them as weave poles. The next day the base was exposed, and none of our dogs had any trouble entering and going through. I now practice occasionally with stick-in-the-ground poles. Do not forget to practice with poles of different colors and striping.

Chapter 20

Life in the Fast Lane

Most obedience exhibitors believe that the step from the open (CDX) class to utility is greater than from novice class into open. In agility, however, the step from novice to open is greater than from open to excellent. Entry-level agility courses are usually quite straightforward, but running your dog at the advanced level requires considerably more training on the part of the dog and much better handling on the part of the exhibitor. It is sometimes difficult to tell the difference between the open and excellent courses at some AKC trials. In fact, I have occasionally had a more challenging course in open than I have had in excellent on the same day. That is never the case in obedience between the open and utility classes.

Obedience exercises are standardized. Most heeling patterns take the form of an L, with a slow in one direction and a fast in the opposite. You rarely get more than three sits before the figure 8, and never less than two. The high jump is always placed somewhere in the middle of the ring in open, and the jumps are always in the same location in the utility ring. There is nothing standardized about agility, however, except for the types of obstacles used on the course.

It is simple to go out and set up an obedience ring. You do not even have to think about it. Setting up an agility course requires a lot of thought and planning. It is beyond the size and scope of this book to go into all the details and handling techniques that you need to train at the advanced level. However, you can get the latest words of wisdom by subscribing to an agility magazine called *Clean Run*. (See Appendix A.) This magazine is filled, from cover to cover, with tips and advice on training, sequences designed to use in a small backyard, and ideas for building equipment. In addition, judges discuss courses they have designed for different competitions and explain how the handler and dog teams fared when on the course. Each issue of *Clean Run* has enough information in it for a month's worth of training. Moreover, the magazine sells agility books of a more technical nature, which will help you prepare for advanced competition and handling.

When you first start training for agility, you teach your dog to negotiate individual obstacles. Then you sequence several obstacles together until your dog can run a simple course. However, you need to teach your dog more than that to compete at the upper levels of the sport. A dog that has earned advanced obedience titles should have no trouble responding to a call-off and handling a lead out. You have already introduced side switches and practiced weaving on the right. In addition to these skills, you need to train your dog in obstacle discrimination and learn how to handle options and traps.

Obstacle Discrimination

Handlers call the obstacles by different names, with the idea that their dogs can discriminate between them. Some dogs eventually learn the names of different obstacles, but many handlers believe that their dogs recognize the names when in fact the dogs are responding to their handlers' signals and body language while running the course. When a dog correctly discriminates between the A-frame placed next to the tunnel, was it because he understood the word "climb," or was it because of the way the dog was handled on the approach to the obstacle? You should certainly attempt to teach your dog the names of the different obstacles, but you may find your dog can also run an entire course with you saying only the words, "Come," "Get out," and "Go." I have heard many handlers, myself included, give an incorrect obstacle command, and the dog still takes the correct obstacle. The reason for this was that the handler's body language told the dog to take the A-frame although the handler said, "Dog walk" by mistake.

When running your dog at the advanced level, you will be facing obstacle discrimination, or traps. A favorite of judges is to place the entrance to a tunnel under the A-frame or dog walk. Like anything else in agility, there is probably no right or wrong way to handle this form of obstacle discrimination since handling in agility is of a more personal nature. In obedience, the regulations force you to carry your hands in a particular way and turn only in a certain direction. The way you handle obstacle discrimination in agility often depends on the type of dog you are running. Knowing how your dog will respond in different situations will help you decide how to handle a trap or option on the course.

Push and Pull

The terms "push" and "pull" in agility do not refer to you pushing your dog or pulling on the leash. If you hear someone say, "I'm going to push my dog out as he leaves the tunnel," that person is referring to having his dog do a "get out." There may be an off-course obstacle facing the tunnel exit, and the handler may choose to push his dog away from it toward the next obstacle in the sequence. Another handler may choose to pull his dog away from the same off-course obstacle, by giving a timely, "Come." The latter handler will be in a different place on the course from the former when he does this. Some dogs push better than they pull. The way to discover your dog's preference is to set up several sequences to see if he responds better to pull than to push. There is often a tunnel under the dog walk or A-frame, so you should practice this form of obstacle discrimination, as well as pull and push, on a regular basis. (See Figures 20-1A, 20-1B, 20-1C, and 20-1D.) In addition, you need to teach your dog to go up the ramp after he exits the tunnel. This type of sequence is also found with regularity at the advanced level. (See Figure 20-2A.) If both the entrance and exit of the tunnel are under the dog walk or A-frame, many dogs miss the ramp and go back into the tunnel entrance. (See Figure 20-2B.) Remember in obedience how, if your dog went into the corner on the first "go out," he would be likely go back to the same place on the second one? Dogs in agility tend to go somewhere they have been before. They become so focused on the tunnel that they do not notice the ramp. For the same reason, you will also need to teach your dog to go into the tunnel once he leaves the ramp of the dog walk or A-frame. (See Figure 20-3A.) You would not expect this to be a problem, but many dogs turn around and go back up the ramp they just descended. (See Figure 20-3B.)

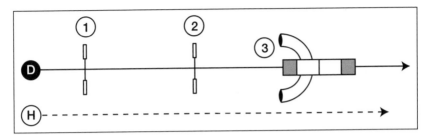

Figure 20-1A. Finding out how well your dog pulls or pushes.
Send him up the A-frame first.

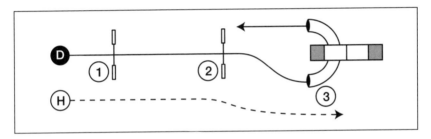

Figure 20-1B. Pull your dog into the tunnel with a "come, tunnel" command.

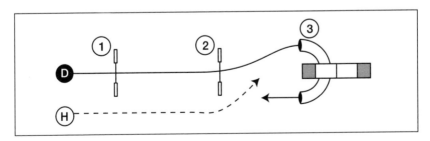

Figure 20-1C. Push you dog into the tunnel with a "get out, tunnel" command.

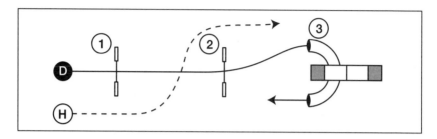

Figure 20-1D. Pull your dog into the tunnel with a switch behind and a "come, tunnel" command.

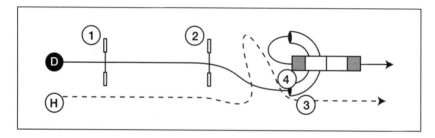

Figure 20-2A. Handler pulls dog into the tunnel, and then sends him up the A-frame.

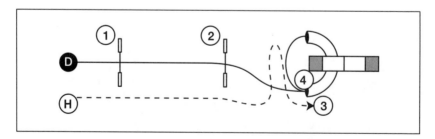

Figure 20-2B. Handler tries to send dog up the A-frame, but the dog returns to the tunnel entrance.

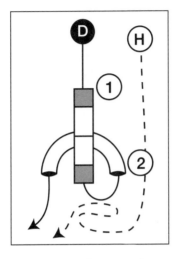

Figure 20-3A. Dog comes down
the ramp of the A-frame
and goes into the tunnel.

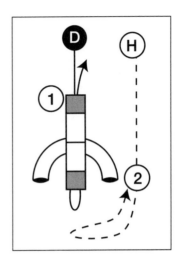

Figure 20-3B. Dog comes down
the ramp of the A-frame, and then
turns around and goes back up it.

Options

Another area where you will use your push and pull is with an option on the course. A favorite option is placing an open tunnel after a jump and then having the dog enter the end opposite than the one he would expect. Knowing if your dog is better at pulling or pushing will help you decide how best to handle this type of challenge when you run the course. (See Figures 20-4A and 20-4B.)

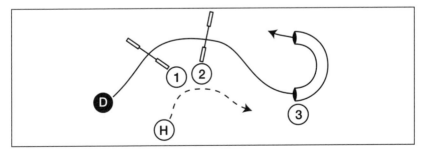

Figure 20-4A. Options: Pulling the dog toward the right tunnel entrance
with a "come, tunnel" command.

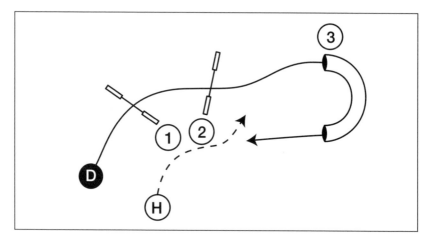

Figure 20-4B. Options: Pushing the dog into the left tunnel entrance with a "get out, tunnel" command.

Angled Approaches to Obstacles

When you first began training, you should have always approached the jumps and obstacles straight on or at a slight angle. When you move to the higher levels of agility, the approach to many of the jumps and obstacles will be at a moderate or steep angle. This is another area where you need to practice.

Proofing

The fact that you need to do some proofing in agility should come as no surprise to anyone who has trained a dog in obedience. Just like in obedience, some dogs will require more proofing than others do. I believe that most dogs are far more focused in agility than they are in obedience. Some time ago at an outside trial, a friend taped my run. When I watched my performance later that day, I was shocked to see another exhibitor throwing a Frisbee parallel to the ring, only ten feet from where my dog was running. Had I been in the obedience ring, I feel sure my dog would have left to chase the Frisbee. As it was, my dog never blinked an eye, she was so focused on the obstacles.

You may need to proof for the judge being on the course. Some dogs are uncomfortable with a judge moving around, particularly a judge walking beside the dog walk or teeter when the dog is on that obstacle. You may need to proof for the count on the pause table. Some dogs anticipate the word "go." You can count out loud yourself or have someone count for you. You may need to count, "5-4-3-2-1 and 5-4-3-2-1 and go." You should have already practiced having your dog sit or lie down on a wet table! Have you practiced with your dog running through a wet chute tunnel? Contact obstacles can become slippery when it rains, so get out the hose. Handlers sometimes fall down during a run. They may be able to pick themselves up again and complete the course, but what happens to the dog? Does he stop when his handler falls down, or does he continue running toward the obstacle to which he was sent as the mishap occurred? It is easy enough to send your dog to a tunnel or contact obstacle and then pretend to fall down and see what he does.

When the adrenaline starts running at a trial, your dog may forget to stay on the contact until you release him. You may need to proof staying on the contact in training by throwing a toy or ball just as your dog reaches the contact area. When you start running your dog at trials, you may quickly discover areas in which you might need to start proofing. In this respect, agility is no different from obedience. Sometimes you have no idea you have a problem exercise until it shows up in the ring. If you have had experience in proofing for obedience performance, you should have no trouble coming up with proofing ideas for agility.

Chapter 21

On Course for Success

Preparing for a Stress-free Agility Trial

Although your dog may be well-trained by the time you enter your first agility trial, there are other factors to take into consideration that will help bring a weekend of agility to a successful conclusion. If you get lost on the way to the show site, you may miss the judge's briefing, which will cause you stress. If you do not make a motel reservation until the last moment, you may have to drive an hour or more to get to the show site. You may get less sleep than you need, and therefore you may not be at your best when it comes time to run your dog.

Before You Enter the Show, Read the Premium List

Many agility trials have entry limits. If this is the case, you may wish to call the trial secretary first to see if there is still space and then send your entry via next-day delivery.

Other events for the same weekend, such as matches and eye clinics, are often advertised in the premium list. Other special events being held at the same time may limit motel availability.

Make Motel Reservations Early

Motels that allow guests to have dogs in the room are getting harder to find, so you should make motel reservations at the same time you send in your entry. Do not find out, just before you are ready to pack the car for the trip, that there is no room at the inn.

> **If you share a room with someone, are you and your dog compatible with your roommate and his or her dog?**

This could be a major disaster if you do not know if the dogs can get along in a confined space. If one of you is a smoker and the other is not, you may end up wishing you had stayed home instead.

Alleviating Dog Stress

If your dog is under stress, he will not work as well as if he is relaxed, so consider practicing the following in the weeks before a trial.

Expose your dog to trial situations where possible.

Practice at the time of day you are likely to show.

> **Remember, if showing early outdoors, grass and contact obstacles may be wet with dew, and your dog may not want to lie down on the table.**

Practice at home by soaking the table with a hose if necessary.

Practice under climatic conditions you are likely to encounter. Turn on a sprinkler to simulate rain and wear a rain suit in which to practice.

Practice with family members around if they plan on going to the trial with you.

> **Does your dog have the stamina to show in several classes on the same day?**

Do not do anything unusual with your dog in the days before the trial. Do not take your dog for a long walk off leash or give your dog his shots. You have a lot of time and money invested in the outcome of the trial. If you take your dog on a walk off leash, he could injure himself. If you take him to the vet for his shots, he might have an allergic reaction to them.

Getting Ready for the Show

Groom Your Dog

Cut his nails and trim hair from his pads if necessary, particularly if the show is indoors on a slick surface, such as carpet.

Make Out a Checklist for the Following:

Pack dog food, water, bowls, treats, medicine, thyroid supplement, heartworm pills, flea spray, bug repellant, diarrhea medicine (Imodium AD or Flagyl), and a book of paper matches in case your dog will not defecate in a strange place. You can use a match as you would a suppository. Moisten the striking end and insert it in the dog's rectum, leaving part of the match extending out of the anus. It should cause most dogs to defecate within seconds. However, should your dog not go, you will be able to remove the match by pulling on the part sticking out of the anus. In addition, do not forget to take a crate along to house your dog at the trial. You will have to leave him unattended when you walk the course. Many exhibitors take a crate to leave at the show site and keep another in their vehicle.

Dog Equipment Needed for the Trip

Flexi® Leash, motivator, agility leash, and rule book.

Handler Clothing and Equipment to Take Along

Ring clothes and shoes, rain suit, warm jacket, extra shoes, sun hat or visor, sunscreen, chair, shade, lunch, soda, and ice chest.

Arriving at the Show Site

If you are not familiar with the show site, it might be advisable to go there the night before if you are driving in from out of town. If the building or grounds are secure, you may wish to unload some of your equipment ahead of time. Take your dog with you to acclimate him to the surroundings.

Check out the location of the rings.

Where is the best place to park?

Is there a shade available?

Day of Show

Where would be the best place to put your kennel or ex-pen, if that is where you plan to keep your dog? Space may be limited. Remember that the number of absentees in your class can affect the time your dog is due in the ring. If the trial offers both standard and games classes, these classes may be running concurrently, and some dogs may be at another ring when it is their turn to run in the class in which you are entered. Although these dogs may not be "absent," they could be missing, and this might affect the time you need to have your dog at ringside.

At events where both obedience and agility are offered and you are faced with a conflict, you must make arrangements with the obedience judge to change your order of showing, prior to the start of the obedience class. If you are going out of turn in obedience, be sure you tell the exhibitor scheduled to follow you. Agility judges are usually more flexible about allowing you to go out of turn than are obedience judges. Agility judges will usually take jump heights out of sequence. If someone has to miss his run due to a conflict with a different class or obedience, most agility judges allow the dog to come back later and have the jump heights reset. However, once the class is over and the course changed, a judge cannot reset a course to accommodate latecomers.

If possible, watch the "run" of several dogs to see if there is a problem area on the course. You may decide to change your strategy.

Keep on top of which handlers have checked in. Who is ahead of you? Know your dog's limitations on warm-up.

Stress can cause your dog to eliminate more frequently. It happens in both obedience and agility. It would be a good idea to teach your dog a "potty" command, and then have him relieve himself immediately before you go in for your run. Do not forget to pick up any piles!

> **Be sure to exercise your dog prior to your time in the ring. You do not want to be eliminated for elimination!**

Reading a Course Layout

At many AKC and NADAC trials, judges often provide a layout of the course for exhibitors to take away and study. This is simply a courtesy, not a requirement, but exhibitors certainly appreciate getting a diagram of their own at which to look. If individual courses are not made available to exhibitors, they will be posted near the ring for handlers to study and trace if they so desire. You should always bring tracing paper along in the event that individual course designs are not handed out. If you need to trace a course, it is often difficult to get through the throng of exhibitors who are standing around studying the posted one. At the first possible moment, pick up the course design sheet or trace the posted one. You should have a good idea of the path your dog will be taking before you walk the course for the first time. When you study the layout, look for potential traps, places where you may need to switch sides, and where the start and finish lines are located.

Walking the Course

Depending on the number of entries in your class, walking the course can be a nightmare. There could be more than fifty people all walking the course at the same time. It is often impossible to get a feel for a course when you have so many bodies getting in your way. Exhibitors often get stepped on or run into by other exhibitors. Judges usually, but not always, give you fifteen minutes or more to walk the course before they call the first dog to the line. Many exhibitors walk the course for that entire time period.

When you are at a trial, you can usually figure out how much time you have to walk the course based on when the judge opens the course for walk-through. When you receive your entry confirmation, it will usually list the time the first dog is due on the line for all classes. In addition, it should say which jump heights run first. If the course opens for walk-through at 7:35 a.m. and the first dog is due on the line at 8 a.m., you will have approximately twenty minutes to walk the course. Most judges clear the course of exhibitors about five minutes before the first dog is brought to the line. If your dog's jump height is the first height to run, you know that you will have no time to waste preparing your dog once the course is closed for walk-through.

If you have ever been to one of the obedience tournaments, you may have laughed as you watched some handlers doing "phantom heeling." Phantom heeling takes place when exhibitors repeatedly practice the heeling pattern without their dogs. They pretend their dogs are at their side and give commands just as they would in the ring. They even praise their phantom dogs for a job well done. Many agility handlers act no differently. When you are walking the course, you will notice handlers calling their imaginary dogs off the start line, running alongside obstacles while giving the appropriate commands and signals, clapping their hands, and bending and twisting their bodies, just as if their dogs are running with them. Before long, you will most likely be doing the same thing!

When I walk the course for the first time, it is to make sure I know the direction the course is taking. The second time I walk it, I start planning my strategy. The third and fourth times I walk it, I visualize running with my dog, but rather than running, I walk. Finally, I run along the course, as I would do if I were competing. If there is still time left, then I move off to the side of the course, close my eyes, and try to visualize the course by repeating the sequence of the obstacles. Just before I expect the judge to have handlers clear the course, I run the course a couple more times, with Phantom!

It is not unusual to see and hear groups of exhibitors discussing points on the course among themselves. They will be asking each other how to best handle a challenge on the course or when to switch sides. It might be beneficial to eavesdrop, if you believe those exhibitors are experienced, and you are there on your own with nobody to give you advice. Sometimes you will hear someone mention a trap that you had not observed on your walk-through.

The Judge's Briefing

At some time before the start of the class, the judge will have a briefing. You should always attend the briefing, as the judge often gives exhibitors timely reminders of things they cannot do when running their dogs. The standard course time (SCT) and yardage is given for all jump heights at this briefing. If there is a pause table on the course, the

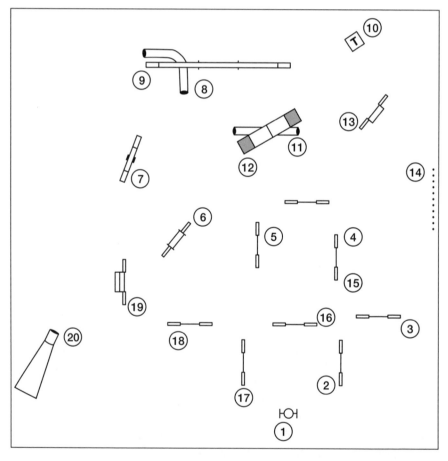

Figure 21-1. Notice how difficult it is to see where to go when the course layout does not show the dog's path.

judge will tell exhibitors how he handles the count and, if there is a choice, whether there will be a "sit" or "down" on the table. The judge will remind exhibitors how many refusals, off-courses, and so forth they may have before they are eliminated and where the start and finish lines are. If you have any questions, this is the time to ask them.

Remembering the Course

It is relatively easy to remember the path the course takes in novice. Novice courses are usually made up of simple loops or figure 8s. However, once you move into the upper levels, it is often difficult to

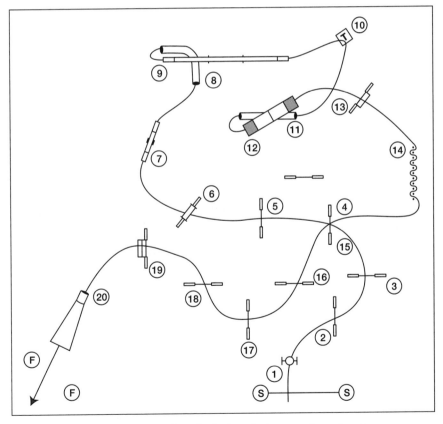

Figure 21-2. Once you draw the dog's path, the course is much easier to remember. Notice the loops and circles. This is an AKC excellent course.

remember the direction of the course because there are so many obstacles and so many different circles and loops. This is the time to make notations of traps. Some courses have a flowing design that you feel the moment you walk the course for the first time. Other courses are choppy. There seems to be neither rhyme nor reason for which way you turn. Choppy courses are much more difficult to remember.

If you are given an individual course layout, the first thing you should do is draw the path around the course your dog has to take. (See Figures 21-1 and 21-2 for an example of how to do this.) The judge may have already done this for you, but if he has not, do it yourself. Once you have drawn the path your dog is to take, rather than look at the obstacle numbers, look to see if there are loops and circles making up the course. There may be a small loop to the right and then a large loop to the left. Next, an inner loop to the left, ending with a large loop to the right. This is one way to remember the course, rather than noticing the individual obstacles. I have a pen with four different colors that I use to mark the course. If the same obstacle is taken more than once, sometimes from a different direction, I change the color I am using at that point. When you take the same obstacle more than once, particularly from the same direction, it is easy to become confused as to where to go next when you are running with your dog.

Study the course shown in Figures 21-1 and 21-2 for a moment and see if you notice some of the challenges and sequences discussed in the previous chapters of this book. Turn to the end of this chapter for the list of challenges on this course.

Courses using contact obstacles are easier to remember than other courses. You can break up these courses into smaller, more manageable parts by remembering sequences such as *start line to the A-frame, A-frame to the dog walk, dog walk to the table*. While your dog is on the table, you will have a moment to regroup. At AKC trials, the pause table is usually in the second third of the course. Finally, your course may end with a sequence such as *the table to the seesaw, the seesaw to the end of the course*. If the course has no contact obstacles, you can identify obstacles such as the tire, chute tunnel, and weave poles to break up the course into more manageable parts. For many exhibitors, the most difficult part of agility is remembering the course.

Running the Course

No matter how you decide to run the course, always have a contingency plan. Things sometimes go wrong, and you end up with your dog on the wrong side of you, or you suddenly forget where to go. When I have forgotten the course, someone who knows nothing about agility will say, "But all the obstacles had numbers. Why didn't you look for the next number on the course?" Unfortunately, it is not that simple. I have not yet figured out how to remember the numbers of the obstacles my dog has already taken. I do not run from number to number, so if I get lost, it is of no help to look at the numbers of the obstacles ahead of me. Occasionally, you can see the number of the obstacle your dog has just taken. If so, you can figure out where to send him next. If you should get lost, stop and call your dog to your side. Providing you are far enough away from the next obstacle in line, you should not receive a penalty for a refusal. If you can regroup, then you can resume running. With luck, you will have enough time to complete the course. Do not forget to cross the finish line. It is not always beyond the last obstacle; sometimes it is off to the side. It is frustrating to have a clean run, only to be eliminated because your dog did not cross the finish line. It has happened to me when I did not pay attention to the finish line and my dog and I left the course without crossing the line, earning a "no time."

If you run your dog in AKC or UKC agility, make sure you know whether it is a "sit" or "down" on the pause table. I have also forgotten that. You will know immediately if you are wrong since the judge will not begin his count. However, this mistake will cost you precious seconds. It is easy to get confused if you are running dogs at different levels under judges who have different table positions.

Training in the Ring

Things may not always go as planned. If your dog made the type of error to cause him to be eliminated, you might consider getting the most out of your run by turning it into a training session. Suppose your dog misses a contact right at the start of the course. If that happened to me, I would insist my dog stay on the next contact for several seconds before I released him to continue his run. I might even touch the bottom of the contact to get him to focus on it. If I had been having trouble on the pause table in training, once my dog was up there in the correct position I might walk up to him and pet him and tell him how good he is. I would reinforce him both verbally and with physical contact. I would do anything I could to help his response at a future trial. Should you do this, the worst thing that could happen is the judge could ask you to leave the course. However, as long as your demeanor is happy, you probably will be allowed to finish your run. If things are really going wrong with your run, with a smile you may wish to thank the judge and then leave the course.

> If you believe your dog needs a drink of water but he will not take one, try this old field trial trick. Put an inch of water in the bottom of a bowl. Then toss one of his favorite treats in the bowl. In order for him to take hold of the treat, he will inevitably take in some water when he opens his mouth. You can repeat this process several times until you think he has had enough to drink.

At the End of the Class

If you have qualified, be sure to take your dog with you when the awards are presented. Remember that you are only one part of the team. Let your partner share in the successful conclusion. There is often a photographer available for pictures. It is nice to have a memento when you finish a title.

Be sure to hold on to any qualifying ribbons until you have received your certificate from the governing body. These ribbons may be your only proof that your dog passed at the trial. Mistakes sometimes happen in recording qualifying scores.

Standard Course Time (SCT)

Paying attention to the time it takes your dog to run the course is something many novice exhibitors never do. However, this knowledge is critical when the moment comes to make a decision to move up to the next level of competition. Many exhibitors starting out in novice are only concerned with whether their dogs run fast enough not to incur time faults. Unless your dog has time to spare at the end of his run, he may not be running fast enough to pass if you move him up to the next level of competition.

At the trial, make a note of the course yardage and standard course time (SCT) and then the time it takes your dog to run the course. Take, for example, an AKC novice standard class where all dogs competing must run at a minimum speed of 2 yards per second with 5 seconds added for the pause table. At your dog's jump height, if a dog's typical path on the course is 132 yards, then the SCT will be 71 seconds. You arrive at this figure by dividing 132 by 2 yards per second, which equals 66 seconds. You then add 5 seconds for the pause table to arrive at a SCT of 71 seconds. In addition, you need to allow a couple of seconds for your dog to get onto the pause table and to assume the correct position before the judge begins his count. For that reason, you will see that your dog will have to run at a speed slightly greater than 2 yards per second in order to make time in novice.

When you move into open, your dog has to run at a faster pace. Accordingly, if you have a large dog that will eventually have to run at 2.5 yards per second in open, then be sure to pay attention to his course time in novice. For him to make time in open, his novice course time for 132 yards should be less than 58 seconds (132 yards ÷ 2.5 yards per second = 53 seconds + 5 seconds for the pause table = 58 seconds SCT). Therefore, if your dog could not run 13 seconds under SCT on our example course (71 seconds − 58 seconds = 13 seconds) then he would be unlikely to make time if you moved him into open.

The same principle holds true when you move from the open to the excellent/elite levels. In AKC open standard, if the typical path for a large dog is 160 yards then the SCT will be 69 seconds (160 yards ÷ 2.5 yards per second = 64 seconds + 5 seconds for the pause table = 69 seconds SCT). In order for your large dog to make time at the excellent level (3 yards per second), he would need to run that open course in less than 58 seconds (160 yards ÷ 3 yards per second = 53 seconds + 5 seconds for the pause table = 58 seconds SCT). If his course time is not considerably under 58 seconds in open, you can see he will have difficulty making time in excellent.

Keep a record of all his course times and a notation if he went off course or had trouble at the pause table, even if he did not qualify because of a downed bar or missed contact. Table troubles or off-courses will have a direct bearing on your dog's time on the course. If you had trouble getting him onto the table or to sit or lie down once he was on the table, then this will add several seconds to his run. If he had an off-course, then this will add yards, as well as seconds. However, if your dog ran clean and, even so, barely made time then you should consider holding him back at the novice/open level until his or your skills improve. Remember that the level of difficulty increases when you move to a higher class.

Even if you determine that your dog is running the novice course at 2.5 yards per second, that really is not fast enough to move up to the open level. In open, a slow response to a call-off or your dog going off course means he will travel farther on the course than the course yardage indicates. Do not forget that course yardage is based on a dog's typical path around the course, not the path taken by your dog. Therefore, take another look at the course yardage and the SCT of 69 seconds with the open level example. Instead of your dog running 160 yards, should he go off course he may end up running 175 yards. If so, in order to still make time he will need to run at 2.75 yards per second (175 yards ÷ 2.75 yards per second = 64 seconds + 5 seconds for the pause table = 69 seconds SCT). Many novice exhibitors are dismayed to discover that their dogs can no longer make time once they move them up to the open or excellent levels. These exhibitors obviously did not take into account their dogs' course time back in novice or open. They only remembered that their dogs got a clean run but then forgot that their dogs' speed is also critical for success when considering moving from one level to another.

Saving the Day

If you are given your own personal copy of the course, do not throw it away after your run, but take it home with you. Later, set up parts of the course or even the entire course to see if, in retrospect, you might run it any differently. If there was a really tricky section of the course that gave you trouble, you could set up the same configuration at home and practice until you and your dog get it right.

I save all my courses in a three-ring binder, starting with a new book each year. Alphabetically, in the front of each binder I list the names of all the judges with the courses in that particular binder. Then, when I enter a show I check to see if I have any courses designed by that judge in the book. In obedience, judges usually use the same heeling pattern, place the articles in the same area of the pile, and locate the jumps in open in the same part of the ring every time they judge. Agility judges often set the same type of trap or start and end with the same type of obstacle. Knowing this can be helpful to the successful outcome of your run.

That old saying "Experience is the best teacher" is very appropriate in agility. The more courses you run, the better you will understand your dog and learn how to handle him. In addition, you will also get more experience in remembering courses, which can often make the difference to the successful outcome of your run.

Did You Find the Challenges on the Course?

This course (Figures 21-1 and 21-2) was chosen at random, from my files of courses that I have run. It presented many of the sequences and challenges for which one should train.

Answers

There is a jumping square at the start of the course. After jump #1, your dog will be faced with an off-course jump, jump #16.

There is an option after jump #3. Your dog has the option to take jump #4 or enter the weave poles.

There is a tempting off-course jump for him to take between #4 and #5, part of a second jumping square.

There is an option after the seesaw, where your dog can either go up the dog walk or through the tunnel.

Your dog has to get on the ramp of the dog walk after coming out of the tunnel.

There is another option after the dog walk, where your dog can either go to the pause table or take the double bar jump, #13.

There is both a trap and an option after the pause table. Your dog has the option to go off course by taking the double bar jump, #13, or he faces the A-frame/tunnel trap.

There is a chance your dog will go off course into the tunnel at #8, rather than make the turn to go up the A-frame. It is difficult to climb the A-frame without taking a run at it.

There is an option after the A-frame. The pause table is more in line with the A-frame than the double bar jump, which is the next obstacle in the sequence, #13.

There is a sharp angle to enter the weave poles.

There is an off-course jump, #3, after the weave poles.

There is another off-course jump, #5, after jump #15.

Jump #16 takes you back into the jumping square once more. The tire becomes an off-course jump.

Jumps #16, #17, and #18 almost make a pinwheel.

There is an option after jump #18. The panel jump, #6, is an off-course jump, or your dog can take the triple, which is the next obstacle in the sequence.

Notice the loops, starting with a figure S starting after the tire and going to the tunnel. Next there is a figure 8 from the table to the weave poles. Then there is almost another S from the weave poles to the finish.

Appendix A

List of Organizations Offering Agility Competitions

Write for rule books.

American Kennel Club (AKC)
5580 Centerview Drive
Raleigh, NC 27606-3390
(919) 233-9767
www.akc.org

United Kennel Club (UKC)
100 East Kilgore Road
Kalamazoo, MI 49001-5593
(616) 343-9020

United States Dog Agility Association (USDAA)
P.O. Box 850995
Richardson, TX 75085-0955
(972) 231-9700

North American Dog Agility Council (NADAC)
HCR 2, Box 277
St. Maries, ID 83861
(208) 689-3803

Australian Shepherd Club of America (ASCA)
6091 East State Highway 21
Bryan, TX 77803-9652
(409) 778-1082

Agility Association of Canada (AAC)
RR#2
Lucan, Ontario
NON 2JO
(519) 657-7636

Agility Magazine

Clean Run Productions, LLC
35 Walnut Street
Turners Falls, MA 01376-2317
(800) 311-6503 or (413) 863-9243
www.cleanrun.com

Useful Web Site

For links to dog agility sites, visit:
www.dogpatch.org

Appendix B

There are many different plans available for making agility jumps. The following are some we modified for ourselves. We have made our jumps 4 feet wide to simplify transporting and moving them. Most people have an arm spread of 4 feet, so this makes it easy to carry 1 or 2 jumps at a time by the uprights. In addition, a 4-foot-wide jump takes up less space than a 5-foot jump. This is a consideration if space is at a premium.

PVC pipe is readily available at most hardware stores. What is usually not available are the pipe fittings and, often, the end caps. My recommendation would be to order all the pipe fittings and end caps from US Plastics. They do sell to the general public and have no minimum order. They also send out their merchandise immediately upon receipt of the order. They have a toll-free number, 1-800-537-9724. Call them to get their catalog before you start to make the jumps/tire jump/table. In addition, they sell barrels that you can use for the chute tunnel.

Jump Uprights

Materials Needed for Making 4 Single Bar Jumps

If you use smaller than 1-inch PVC pipe, the pipe is likely to warp. If you use larger than 1-inch pipe, you will be unable to use a PVC pipe cutter, which simplifies construction. You can use a hacksaw to cut the PVC pipe, but it takes a lot more time than using the pipe cutter.

You Need to Buy:

PVC pipe cutter (optional)
PVC pipe glue
8 (10-foot) lengths of 1-inch i/d, schedule 40 PVC pipe. Four of the 10-foot lengths will be used to make 8 jump bars; the other 4 lengths will be used to make the jumps.
Colored plastic electrical tape to stripe the bars. Colored duct tape is not recommended. If you leave your jumps outside, the sun will fade the duct tape and turn it brittle. You will need to replace it often. Electrical tape holds up much better than duct tape.
48 (¼-inch × 3½-inch) threaded-end bolts with nuts, to use for bar supports. You can use fewer nuts and bolts if you don't mind moving the bar supports whenever you change jump heights.

From US Plastics, Order:

8 (1-inch) 4-way Ell pipe fittings, which will be used to make the bases of the jumps. Note that this is *not* a 4-way cross.
24 (1-inch) end caps. Caps are not essential, but they prevent dirt and grass from getting into the pipe. You will need 3 caps for each upright.
If you wish, you can make 1 jump that uses a 5-way cross. This style of jump is not as stable as the one recommended above. However, you can use it as the first section of a double bar jump because the feet are smaller, and it can be used for dogs that jump 8 and 12 inches. If you decide to make this style of jump, you will need to order two 5-way crosses from US Plastics to make two uprights and buy 4 additional (1-inch) end caps.

To Construct the Jumps

Cut the pipe into the following lengths:
8 (30-inch) pieces (use 2 [10-foot] lengths) to make the 8 jump uprights

4 (44-inch) pieces* to make the cross braces. The cross brace makes the jump very stable. If you wish, you can cut 1 of the cross braces to 41 inches. Then you can place the base of 1 upright inside another base to make a (double bar) spread jump for dogs that jump 16 inches or more.

16 (8-inch) pieces* for the feet of the upright, 2 pieces per side

*Cut 2 (44-inch) pieces and 4 (8-inch) pieces out of each 10-foot piece of pipe.

8 (52-inch) pieces (out of the other 4 [10-foot] lengths) to make the jump bars. You will need 2 bars for each jump.

(Never throw away unused pieces of PVC pipe. You never know when an odd piece may come in useful.)

If you use a 5-way cross to make the base, you will not need a cross brace. Instead, cut the pipe into 2 (4½-inch) pieces, 4 (5½-inch) pieces, and 2 (7½-inch) pieces. The longest section of the pipe will add stability to the upright. The shortest section can face the cross brace of the regular jumps and will make the correct spread of the double bar jump for the 8-inch dog.

To Assemble the Jumps

Glue a 30-inch piece into the center hole (A) of each 4-way Ell pipe fitting (see Figure B-1) to make the upright. (If you are using a 5-way cross, glue a 30-inch upright into the center hole of the 5-way cross.) Next, glue 1 (8-inch) piece into each end of the pipe fitting (B) to make the feet of the base. Do not glue the 44-inch cross brace into hole (C) since you may wish to remove the cross brace for jump storage or transportation. (If you are making an upright using the 5-way cross, assemble the pieces as follows: Glue 1 (5½-inch) piece of pipe opposite the 7½-inch pipe. Then glue the other 5½-inch piece opposite the 4½-inch piece. This will form the base of one upright.)

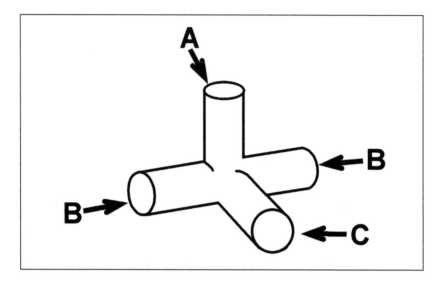

Figure B-1. Four-way Ell pipe fitting.

On the upright, at 90 degrees to the hole for the cross brace (C), drill 5 (¼-inch) holes. (If you are using the 5-way cross, then drill the holes at 90 degrees to the longest piece of the base.) Start the first hole 6½ inches up from the ground, and then drill a hole every 4 inches up to 22½ inches. Drill 1 hole below the 8-inch hole for a second bar if you train a small dog. To line up the holes, you may wish to use the lettering on the pipe as a guide. Before you glue in the uprights, be sure the lettering is where you want to drill the holes. If you anticipate jumping your dog at 26 inches, buy 8 additional end bolts and nuts. Drill another hole in the upright at 24½ inches.

Glue caps onto all the open ends of the jump uprights. Stripe the jump bars with the plastic tape. You can stripe them diagonally or vertically—every few inches.

Tire Jump

Because the tire jump needs to be stable in windy conditions, you should make it out of 1¼-inch PVC pipe. If you use 1¼-inch PVC pipe, you will have to cut the pipe with a hacksaw. You can make the frame out of 1-inch pipe, but it is not recommended. The directions are the same except you will substitute 1-inch pipe and pipe fittings and can use your PVC pipe cutter. Because you need to cut very few pieces of PVC pipe when making the tire frame, using a hacksaw to cut 1¼-inch pipe should not be too time consuming.

Materials Needed for Making the Tire Frame

3 (10-foot) sections of 1¼-inch i/d, schedule 40 PVC pipe
4 feet of ⅝-inch rebar (R), to add weight to the jump base
8 feet of ⅜-inch (bulk) bungee cord (BC) and 4 (⅜-inch) bungee hooks. Cut the bungee cord in half to make 2 bungee cords.
4 (1⅜-inch) #10 screw eyes (S)
1 (2¹⁄₁₆-inch) steel ceiling hook (H)
1 medium S hook

From US Plastics, Order:

2 (1¼-inch) 4-way Ell pipe fittings (the same as you used for the jumps, but in a larger size)
4 (1¼-inch) end caps (E)
2 (1¼-inch) elbow connectors (F)

Materials Needed for Making the Tire

7 feet of ABS 4-inch-diameter non-perforated flexible sewer pipe. This pipe comes in both white and black. You may have to buy a 10-foot piece and cut it.
3 (¼-inch) toggle bolts (T). You will discard the bolts and replace them with the eye bolts.
3 (¼-inch × 3-inch) eye bolts (B)
3 fender washers (W), ⅜-inch opening, making at least 1-inch total diameter
4 (8-inch) nylon cable ties (C)

3 feet of medium-weight double link chain. The links should be 1-inch links.

Duct tape (D)

Two rolls of colored plastic electrician's tape (E)

To Construct the Frame

Cut the pipe into the following lengths:

2 (5-foot) pieces. This will make the two uprights (A).

2 (4-foot) pieces. This will make the top bar and the cross brace (C).

4 (18-inch) pieces. This will make the feet of the frame (B).

To Assemble the Frame (see Figure B-2)

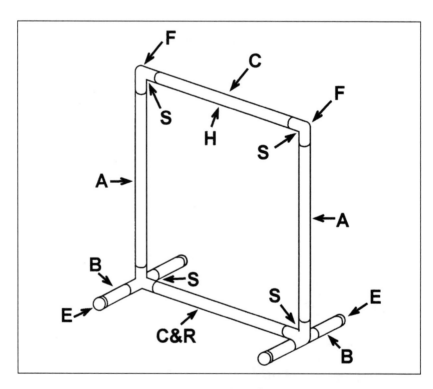

Figure B-2. Tire jump frame.

Glue 2 (18-inch) pieces into both ends of the 4-way Ell pipe fitting (B) (see Figure B-1); then glue 1 of the 5-foot pieces into the center hole (A). Repeat. Glue an elbow (F) onto each end of 1 of the 2 (4-foot) pieces (C) to make the top of the frame. Place the piece of rebar (R) inside the other 4-foot section of PVC pipe (C) that will be used as the lower cross brace. Connect this cross brace to the 2 feet, but do not glue unless you know you will never need to transport the frame. Place the other 4-foot section with the elbows on top of the uprights, and push down. Glue only if you will not be transporting the frame. Drill a hole on the underside of the top bar in the center (H), and screw in the ceiling hook. The tire will be suspended by the chain from this hook. Drill a hole in the underside corner of both elbows (S) and screw in 2 of the screw eyes. Drill a hole at the base of each upright on the inside just above the cross brace (S), and screw in the other 2 screw eyes. The bungee hooks holding the tire will attach to these eyes, top and bottom, to hold the tire steady. Glue the caps (E) to the ends of the feet.

To Assemble the Tire (see Figure B-3)

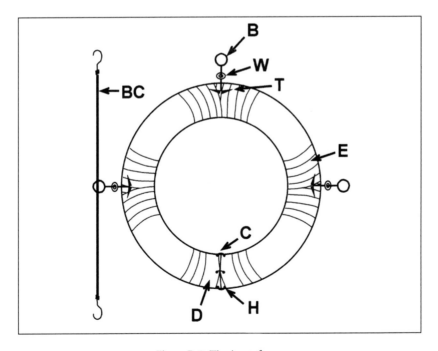

Figure B-3. Tire jump frame.

The AKC tire has a 24-inch opening. The one used in USDAA has a 17- to 20-inch opening. You should train your dog using the smaller diameter tire.

Cut the sewer pipe to approximately 84 inches with a razor/utility knife or hacksaw. Make sure the ridges meet smoothly. Butt the ends together and punch 4 holes on each side (H), about ½-inch in from the edge where it joins, on the top, bottom, and each side. Thread a cable tie (C) through the holes at the top, bottom, and sides and join the pipe together to form a circle. Tighten gradually. Cut off the excess cable. You may need to shape the pipe to make it round.

Use duct tape (D) to cover and reinforce the area where the pipe is joined with the cable ties. This area will be at the bottom of the tire when it is hanging on the frame. Wrap the tire with electrician's tape (E). Punch three holes in the tire at 12, 3, and 9 o'clock. Make the holes just large enough to pass the toggles through. Be sure the duct-taped area is opposite 12 o'clock. Place the washer (W) on the eyebolt (B) and screw the toggle bolt (T) on after the washer. Push each toggle through into the tire, make sure it opens, and then screw the eyebolt down until it is held snugly against the washer. Slide one end of the bungee cord through the 9 o'clock eyebolt and the other piece of bungee cord through the 3 o'clock eyebolt (BC). Attach the 4 bungee hooks to the ends of the cord. Attach 1 end of the S hook to the eyebolt at the top of the tire and the other end to the last link of the double link chain. Hook the chain to the ceiling hook (H). Attach the bungee hooks to the 4 eye bolts (S), and adjust the height of the tire by raising or lowering the chain. The height of the tire is measured from the inside of the bottom of the tire to the ground. Place pieces of electrical tape on the links of the chain and mark on them the height of the tire.

The Pause Table

Like the tire and the jumps, the table is adjusted for the height of the dog. If you know you will never need to adjust the height of the table, you can use PVC pipe for the legs. The PVC pipe fits so tightly into the pipe fittings that it is almost impossible to remove even if it has not been glued. If you plan to train with dogs of different jump heights, make the height of the table adjustable by using wooden dowels or steel closet rods for the legs.

Materials Needed for Making the Table Base

2 (10-foot) pieces of 1-inch i/d, schedule 40 PVC pipe (B). This amount of pipe is for the base only and does not include material for the legs.

1 (10-foot) piece of rebar (R), cut into 4 identical lengths. (In place of rebar you can always fill the PVC pipe with sand.)

Materials Needed to Make the Table Legs

Either use 1-inch PVC pipe, like you used to make the base, or you can use 1¼-inch wooden dowels or 1¼-inch steel closet rods. See section under table construction for the amount of material to buy, based on the height of the table needed for the size of dog you are training.

Materials Needed for the Tabletop

1 piece of ½- or ⅝-inch exterior plywood, 36 inches ✕ 36 inches
8 (2¾-inch ✕ ¼-inch) flat head bolts, lock washers, and nuts
Paint for the tabletop
Silica for adding to the paint, to make the tabletop non-slip

From US plastics, Order:

8 (1-inch) 3-way Ells

To Construct the Table

Cut the pipe into the following lengths:
8 (30-inch) pieces (B)

How to Figure the Length of Legs

You have to allow for the height of the two 3-way Ells, how far the legs insert into the Ells, and the thickness of the tabletop. The length you cut the legs amounts to the table height less 3¼ inches. Wooden dowels only come in 3-foot lengths, while closet rods come in 4-, 6-, and 8-foot lengths.

For 8-Inch Table Height:

4 pieces, 4¾ inches long. You may find you have some pieces of PVC pipe left over from your jump construction. If not, some home improvement centers sell short pieces of pipe. If you plan on using wooden dowels or closet rods, you will need 1 wooden dowel or 1 (4-foot) closet rod.

For 16-Inch Table Height:

4 pieces, 12¾ inches long. You will need 5 feet of PVC pipe. If you plan on using wooden dowels or closet rods, you will need 2 wooden dowels or 1 (6-foot) closet rod.

For 24-Inch Table Height:

4 pieces, 20¾ inches. You will need to buy 10 feet of PVC pipe. If you plan on using wooden dowels or closet rods, you will need 4 wooden dowels or 1 (8-foot) closet rod.

For Interchangeable Table Heights, You Will Need the Following:

8-Inch and 16-Inch Table:
2 wooden dowels: Cut each dowel into 2 (4¾-inch) and 2 (12¾-inch) sections. 1 (6-foot) closet rod, and cut 4 (4¾-inch) and 4 (12¾-inch) sections.

16-Inch and 24-Inch Table:
4 wooden dowels: Cut each dowel into 1 (12¾-inch) and 1 (20¾-inch) piece, or 2 (6-foot) closet rods and cut each into 2 (12¾-inch) pieces and 2 (20¾-inch) pieces.

To Assemble the Table Base (see Figure B-4)

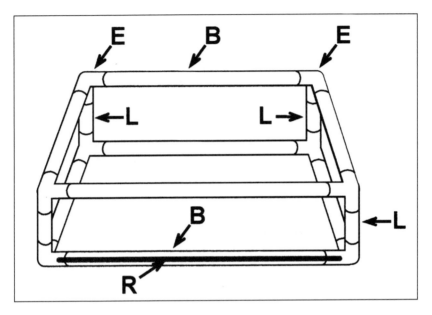

Figure B-4. Table base.

Place the 4 pieces of rebar (R) into 4 of the 30-inch pieces of PVC pipe (B). Glue the 4 pieces of 30-inch pipe (B) with rebar (R) inside, into the ends of four 3-way Ells (see Figure B-5) to form a square. This will make the base of the table. Repeat, using the other 30-inch pieces of pipe and the other 3-way Ells. This second square will make the base on which to set the tabletop (see Figure B-6). Eventually, the legs (L) will attach these 2 square frames to each other. The legs will fit into the third hole (E) in the pipe fitting to form a cube.

If you make the legs out of wooden dowels or closet rods, you can always wrap the ends of the legs with a couple of layers of electrician's tape. This will make the legs fit a little tighter into the 3-way Ell pipe fittings (E).

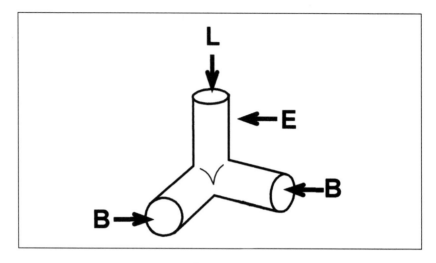

Figure B-5. Three-way Ell pipe fitting for table base.

To Assemble the Tabletop (see Figure B-6)

You will need a ¼-inch drill bit. First, mark the tabletop where you need to drill the 8 holes (H)—3 inches in from each corner and 1½ inches in from the edge. Attach the tabletop to the upper frame using C clamps. Make sure the top is sitting squarely on the upper base. Make sure the holes in the upper pipe fittings (E) are pointed away from the tabletop so that you can insert the legs. Drill 8 holes through the table-top and the PVC pipe. Use the drill to widen the outer part of the hole so that the head of the bolt is counter-sunk and not sticking up above the surface of the table. Attach the tabletop with the bolts, the lock washers, and nuts (S). Insert the legs (L) in the PVC base, and then attach the tabletop to the legs. Paint the tabletop. Add silica to the paint. You may have to use several coats.

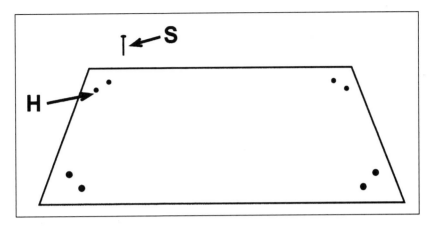

Figure B-6. Tabletop.

Flexible Weave Poles

Design courtesy of Gordon Simmons-Moake, Flash Paws Agility Club of Houston, TX.

These weave poles will work with any base that accepts ¾-inch PVC pipe. You may need to modify the design slightly depending on the height of the post on the base that holds the weave poles. The materials should be available at any home improvement center. You should not attach guide wires to this type of pole.

For 12 Poles, You Need to Buy:

1 (10-foot × ¾-inch) sch. 40 PVC pipe
4 (10-foot × ¾-inch) plastic, flexible electrical conduit (blue, ribbed)
4 (10-foot × ½-inch) CPVC pipe. This is not the same as PVC.
12 (½-inch) CPVC end caps
1 (³⁄₁₆-inch × 23-inch) plastic electric fence insulating pipe. (Dark green with small holes. It should barely fit inside the conduit and PVC, and the CPVC should fit inside the insulator.)
24 (#6 × ¾-inch) pan-head machine screws

To Construct the Poles, Cut:

12 pieces ¾-inch PVC, 7 inches long
12 pieces ½-inch CPVC, 34½ inches long
12 pieces blue conduit, 32¼ inches long
12 pieces green insulator, about 1¾ inches long

To Assemble 1 Pole (see Figure B-7)

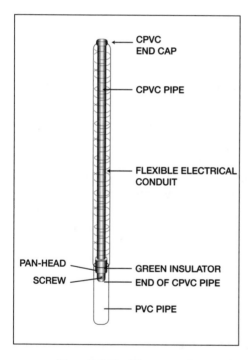

Figure B-7. Flexible weave pole.

Glue an end cap onto one end of the CPVC pipe. Push the piece of green insulator halfway into one end of the blue conduit. Slide a piece of PVC pipe over the stub of the protruding insulator. This piece of PVC pipe forms the base of the weave pole and adjoins the more flexible blue insulator. Slide a piece of CPVC pipe, open end first, inside the blue conduit. The end cap will prevent the CPVC pipe from sliding all the way through to the bottom. If you use these flexible poles on a base that uses posts to hold the poles, if the CPVC pipe went all the way to the bottom it would prevent the base of the pole from slipping over the post. Drill a ³⁄₃₂-inch hole through the PVC pipe ½-inch below where the PVC and conduit meet. Use a power screwdriver to screw in the pan-head screw, which should pass through the PVC, insulator, and

CPVC pipe. Rotate the pole a quarter of a turn and then drill a second hole ½-inch below the first and add another screw.

The Food Tube

Go to a home improvement center and buy 1 foot of clear plastic tubing ⅝-inch ID, ⅞-inch OD. In addition, buy a package of ⅞-inch rubber feet made for the end of chair legs. Cut the plastic in 2 to make 2 tubes. Drill a number of ¼-inch holes in the plastic and put 1 cap on each end. You can fill the tube with treats and then take off 1 of the caps to give your dog his reward. Your dog will be able to smell the food but not eat it. Alternatively, cap each end and then make a diagonal cut across the plastic with a razor knife and fill the tube with treats. When you want to get some food out, all you do is twist the tube, and the food will pop out.

Another solution is to take a small, plastic food-storage bowl with a lid and drill a number of holes in both the lid and the bowl. Your dog will be able to smell the food, but he will not be able to get to it unless you are there to reward him. Whichever type of food tube you make, first introduce it to your dog by placing it on the ground or up on your target platform before you use the tube for training. Allow your dog to sniff it and then let him see you remove the food and give it to him.

Instead of making a food tube, you can purchase food tubes in various sizes from *Clean Run* magazine.

Index

Kay Guetzloff and her Heelalong Border Collies—"Lava": OTCH Heelalong Molten Lava UDX, MX, MXJ, PT;"Wyn": Heelalong Wynd Dancer CDX, OA, OAJ; "Sweep": OTCH Heelalong Chimney Sweep UDX, AX, AXJ; "Kite": CH/OTCH Heelalong Hi Flying Red Kite UDX, MX, MXJ, PT (photo by Shary Singer).

For more than thirty years, **Kay Guetzloff's** life has gone to the dogs. Kay is best known as the breeder of Heelalong Border Collies, one of which—OTCH Heelalong Chimney Sweep UDX, AX, AXJ—is, at this writing, the most winning dog in the history of the sport of AKC obedience. Kay's husband, Dick, trained and handled Sweep in obedience. When Sweep reached the tender age of twelve years, she started a new career with Kay in the agility ring, earning her AX and AXJ titles.

When Kay immigrated to the United States from England in 1965, one of her first orders of business was to buy a dog. Siebe Konigin von Mayrhofen UDT, a Longhaired Dachshund, was one of Kay's many obedience stars. In that era, dog training classes were rare, and dog training seminars were almost nonexistent. Kay borrowed a couple of dog training books from the library and a year later entered her first AKC obedience trial. Kay and Siebe returned home with High Scoring Dog honors, earning 199.5 points out of a possible 200. Kay was hooked on obedience. Exactly one year later Siebe had earned the highest AKC performance title of that time, Utility Dog Tracker (UDT). When Kay moved back to England in 1969, she took Siebe with her. After a stint in quarantine, Siebe went on to win an obedience challenge certificate and qualify for the Crufts Obedience Championship at the world's premier dog show. This was an unheard-of honor for a Dachshund.

When Kay returned to the United States, her interest in obedience continued. Kay's first Obedience Trial Champion was also a Longhaired Dachshund, OTCH Mayrhofen Olympischer Star L TD, Gretl, who was the first hound to achieve that honor. Since that time, seven more of Kay's dogs have become obedience champions, and Kay has the distinction of having put obedience titles on dogs out of all seven AKC groups.

Now Kay owns the Heelalong Dog Obedience and Agility School in San Angelo, Texas. She and her husband have taught competition obedience classes and seminars since 1977. The Guetzloffs have won many national obedience honors with their dogs. More recently, Kay started competing in agility, where she has used her training knowledge to earn multiple agility titles, including two MX and MXJ titles. She has also helped some of her obedience students get a start in the sport of agility. In all, Kay and her dogs have earned seventy-seven obedience titles and forty agility titles.